1001

AFFIRMATIONS

BY

HERBERT P. WINDSCHITL

© 2003 by Herbert P. Windschitl. All rights reserved.

No part of this book may be reproduced, stored in a retrieval system, or transmitted by any means, electronic, mechanical, photocopying, recording, or otherwise, without written permission from the author.

ISBN: 1-4033-5455-3 (e-book)
ISBN: 1-4033-5456-1 (Paperback)
ISBN: 1-4033-5457-X (Dust Jacket)

Library of Congress Control Number: 2002093286

This book is printed on acid free paper.

Printed in the United States of America
Bloomington, IN

1stBooks – rev. 07/22/03

The daisies on the cover were selected for a number of reasons. The daisy was known in Old English, as a likeness to a tiny sun surrounded by white rays. The oxeye daisy is a species of chrysanthemum native to Europe. It also refers to a days eye.
Daisies blossum like an eye, close at night and open at dawn. A tradition says that it was carried to America in hay brought to feed the horses of General Burgoyne's army during the Revolutionary War. <u>Compton's Encyclopedia</u> 1998. This daisy's activity is almost like human existence.

Enjoy the affirmations and stories designed to give direction in some critical areas of your life. The quipps, interrelationships, behavior modifications, fifteen minute meditations and goal setting section will help develop your personal goals in life. This is especially written for teachers, writers, youth leaders, public speakers, priests, ministers, executives, husbands and wives, students, children and anyone on a self improvement track to influence other people around them. Many sales people will find this book beneficial.

Any acknowledgments not recorded here can be acknowledged in writing with subsequent printings. The author does not claim to have written all of these affirmations but does reserve the credit for collecting them and sharing their insights about life with the reader for educational purposes. This work is done in union with thousands of teachers and parents across America that want the human family to grow. Used with permission.

OPEN A LIFE AND COME ALIVE

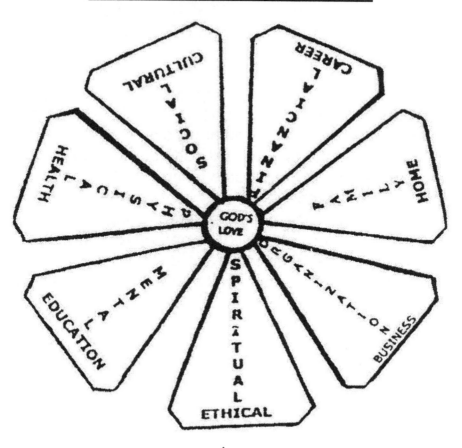

PREFACE

1001 Affirmations is a selection of affirmations, quipps, interrelationships, behavior modifications, fifteen minute meditations and goal setting section that are designed to help add direction to your life and achieve what you personally want. Many affirmations have been taken from other people's lives.

From this information formulate your own direction in the seven areas of your life; mental, spiritual, physical, social, financial, family and business.

**DEDICATED
TO MY WIFE BERNIE
CHILDREN
AND GRANDCHILDREN**

**HONORARY DEDICATION
Holy Family**

INTRODUCTIONS

Over 25 years I have had the honor of substituting in the classrooms of many great teachers. Every teacher somehow picks up an affirmation or two they proudly display in their classrooms. I often thought these affirmations should be more widely circulated that others may be able to enrich their lives.

I have always somehow been fascinated by the one liners or paragraphs that stimulate us to achieve goals beyond our dreams, or just calm us down to see what life is all about. When we read a good book we can pick up some good positive expressions. Many times it takes hours to come up with one expression that really fits into our lives.

In my full time teaching experiences for 14 years and some 30 years sales experiences I've depended many times on some of these affirmations. With these thoughts in mind, I'd like to share as many as I can recall from notes I kept over a period of time.

Every affirmation in this repertory might not appeal to you so I encourage you to select the ones that you like most or helps the friends you wish to influence. These quiet, quick, decisive statements bring an immediate smile and firm conviction to move ahead with your life. Once over a mental block you need to repeat these statements to reinforce your true convictions.

1001 AFFIRMATIONS

These affirmations are not in any particular order just like road blocks in life do not come in any specific pattern. Check off the ones that help you the most and get in the habit of repeating them dozens of times. I'm sure you'll find these statements strong and decisive in getting to the heart of a difficult situation.

The Good Lord used many affirmations to move us to a firmer grasp of helping us solve our personal problems. So let it be with us.

<u>As you scan these affirmations you can come to your own conclusions of what you believe in. Then write your own affirmations for yourself. Affirmations are counted as individual statements, paragraphs, sets of an idea or poems.</u>

<u>A note of information</u>: The idea of the 1001 Affirmations came out of a visit to Kyoto, Japan in the early 50's when I was in the Korean Conflict. I visited a temple of Sanjusangen-do, founded in 1164, where 1001 gilded life like wooden statues of the Japanese deity Kannon were lined up.

CONTENTS

Preface v
Saints 3
General Affirmations 5
A Sense of Class 7
Let It Be Done 10
Rules of the World 15
Blessings 16
Master Teacher 17
A B C's of Happiness 18
A B C's of Selling 26
Four Wants In Life: Time Management; Basic Needs;
Success Essentials 27
100 of Life's Activities 32
Teacher Motivation 36
Twenty Two Suggestions For Success 40
Sales Motivation 42
10 Commandments of God 49
Nicene Creed 50
Meditations of Faith 51
Ten Rules of Success 55
Am I A Builder? 63
Happiness 65
Point of View 72
Signs of Workaholism 79
You're Right 80
Anyway 81
Good Sport Prayer Cardinal Cushing 82
Saint Benedict Medal 83
Mother 92

Challenges	93
A Father's Prayer	94
Pope John II's Thoughts of Money	97
Seven Laws of Success	102
In Our Books	107
Reaching Out	108
Prayer for Peace	114
Time	115
Love	116
Success	119
Alcohol Kills	120
Be Bold	121
Be an Angel	123
Ten Secrets To Success and Inner Peace	124
Family Affirmations	125
Goal Setting	128
Authors Motto and Leaders Prayer	130
My Personal Goals	132
Celebrity and Author Affirmations	133
My Dream List	145
My Directions	149
List Your Personal Affirmations and Goals	150
Appendix	170
Children Learn What They Live With	171
All I Really Need To Know I Learned In Kindergarten	172
Desiderata	173
About The Author	175

Any good that I shall do, let me do it now, for I shall not pass this way again.

Oh Lord, help me keep myself out of other people's business.

Lord, add direction to my confusion.

What you believe yourself to be you are.

Ignorance is Public Enemy # 1.

I am still learning.
Know lots talk little.

Inspect what you expect.

I expect to see people and I will.

Don't put off until tomorrow what you can do today.

A man's reach must exceed his grasp or what's a heaven for. Browning

My job is to instruct the ignorant.

We meet all our friends in church every Sunday.

The Two great commandments are: Love God and Love Neighbor.

Guide me O Lord to act my age.

G.K. Chesterton once said. "It's good to be in hot water occasionally. It keeps you clean."

What I do today is important because I am exchanging a day of my life for it. Hugh Mulligan

One day is worth two tomorrow's. Ben Franklin

Hell is for people who want it.

Prayer is the only way to heaven.

Work Habits:

1. Concentrate, 2. Work steadily, 3. Plan ahead, 4. Be accurate, 5. Be careful, 6. Be friendly and pleasant.

Winners have certain attitudes in common:

1. They are willing to pay the price.
2. They are willing to make a personal commitment.
3. They are willing to accept personal responsibility.

In short, a winner thinks like a winner and acts like a winner.

SAINTS

What all Saints have in common: (*Catholic Digest 1990*) 1. All Saints sin. 2. All Saints suffer. 3. All Saints Pray. 4. All Saints are humble. 5. All Saints strive to love. 6. All Saints challenge society. 7. All Saints trust in God. 8. All Saints want to be Saints.

Observation of people: 1. Bad people are generally hard on others and easy on themselves. 2. Good people are generally hard on others and hard on themselves. 3. Saints are hard on themselves and easy on others.

A good education no one can take away from you.

It's more important to love than it is to hate. When love ends hate moves in.

It's not so much who is right but what is right.

Live and help live helps you to stand on your own two feet.

One good father is worth a hundred school masters: Strict discipline; tempered by love; worked at a job; Prayed at church.
Did the best at raising a family; Firmness crept in a voice; Fear that grasp the heart.
(17TH Century English proverb.)

Herbert P. Windschitl

"I say to you today, my friends, so even though we still face the difficulties of today and tomorrow I still have a dream." 1963 Dr. Martin Luther King. Remember the message as we remember the man.

Yesterday is history; Tomorrow a mystery; Today is a gift from God.
That's why they call it—The Present.

St. Cyril of Jerusalem: The dragon is by the side of the road. Watching those who pass. Beware lest he devour you. We go to the Father of Souls. But it is necessary to pass by the dragon. Flannery O'Connor

Joshua: 24:15 I don't know about you my friend but as for this house we shall serve the Lord.

It's one thing to accumulate possessions but it takes a greater person to appreciate what you have accumulated.

I don't have enough time to deal with mediocre advice or ideas. Life is too short not to depend on some verifying authority.

There is nothing Lord that you and I together can't solve.

CHILDREN: Tired of being harassed by your parents? Act now, move out, get a job, pay your own bills while you still know everything.

If you are grouchy, irritable or just plain mean, there will be a $10.00 charge for putting up with you.

General Affirmations

Home Rules
If you sleep on it; make it up. If you wear it; hang it up. If you eat off it; clean it up. If you open it; close it. If you empty it; fill it up. If it rings; answer it. If it howls; feed it. If it cries; love it.

We're in the people building business.

If you don't fall for something you'll fall for anything.

Let learning take you around the world.

A person who does not understand salesmanship misses half of life.

If you want a perfect spouse make sure you are perfect yourself.

Church attendance, family reunions or class reunions help us to grow old gracefully.

God has never refused me a prayer yet. He didn't always give me what I wanted but very often has given me something better.

Parents haven't always given us the gifts we wanted but if we reflect on their decisions we find that their gifts were given out of love and concern for our long range growth and development.

Herbert P. Windschitl

If you think work is a pain in the neck, try life without any work.

Where you stand depends on where you sit.

The secret of getting ahead is getting started.

If doing homework is a crime is there enough evidence to convict?

There are three kinds of people in life: A. Those that make things happen; B. Those who watch what happens; C. Those who wonder what happened.

Stress reduction: A. Get more sleep; B. Eat healthy; C. Exercise 10-15 minutes daily; D. Breathe deeply; E. Pray more fervently.

When I leave this world I want Jesus's Church to have the last word.

WORDS: A. The dictionary is the word of man. B. The Bible is the word of God. C. The seed catalog is the word of nature.

There comes a time in life when we must do our own loving, praying, and working.

I can; I will; I must. I've done it before I can do it again.

A Sense Of Class

Class never runs scared. It is surefooted and confident. It can handle whatever comes along.

Class has a sense of humor. It knows that a good laugh is the best lubricant for oiling the machinery of human relations.

Class never makes excuses. It takes its bumps and learns from mistakes.

Class knows good manners are nothing more than a series of petty sacrifices.

Class bespeaks an aristocracy that has nothing to do with money.

Some extremely wealthy people have no class at all while others who are struggling to make ends meet are loaded with it.

Class is real, you can't fake it.

The person with class makes you feel comfortable because he is comfortable with himself.

If you have class you have it made.

If you don't have class, no matter what else you have, it doesn't make any difference.

Inspiration of class from Iowa University football.

_____

Success is yours when starting with an "A".
Avoid working for power or money.
Be honest, reliable, faithful and aggressive.
Choose your friends carefully.
Don't be afraid to take risks.
Establish goals and work systematically toward achieving them.
Free rides don't exist.
_____Unknown._____

Herbert P. Windschitl

Herbert P. Windschitl

Let It Be Done

Have confidence that you can make a difference.
Invite constructive criticism.
Just doing enough to get by won't get it done.
Keep from making excuses.
Listen, learn and always work to improve your mind.
Mean what you say and say what you mean.
Never give up on your dreams.
Only one person can control you and that's you.
Pray- Quality not quantity.

Respect others.
Sometimes slow down and smell the roses.
Treat others with respect, and they will respect you.
Use assests wisely. Voice you opinions.
Work as hard as possible, without forgetting your loved ones.
Expect obstacles, but accept challenges.
You are in charge of your own actions.
Zap obstacles and reach for the stars.
Western Graphics Corporation

When a problem in life becomes unbearable you can laugh, cry or pray. You have a choice.

The real test of a Christian is what you will do the rest of the week after Sunday.

Most families are like a box of chocolates. Mostly sweet but some come with nuts in them.

Your mother does not work here so you'll have to pick up after yourself.

People are about as happy as they make up their minds to be. Lincoln

Success in life has three bones; A wish bone; backbone and a funny bone.

When something can be read without effort, great effort has gone into its writing. Enrique Jardiel Poncela

Formula for failure; Try to please everyone. Garrison Keilor

Don't miss out on a blessing because it isn't packaged the way you expect.

I cannot do everything; but I can do something. Because I cannot do everything I will not refrain from doing something that I can do.

Teachers change the world one child at a time.

Dear program; Drop everything and READ.

Those who cannot remember the past are condemned to repeat it. Santayana

Herbert P. Windschitl

To know nothing of what happened before you were born is to remain forever a child. Cicero

People seldom improve when they have no other model but themselves to copy from. Oliver Goldsmith

Marriage is Love and Respect; Take life one bite at a time.

Education is learning to find yourself. Education is the art of finding your place in life and then some.

The Bar is the place where the BULL keeps on going and never stops.

We can choose to throw stones; To stumble on them; To climb over them; or To build with them.

Do the right thing even if everyone disagrees. Do everything right every time in every way no matter how you feel.

Sometimes in life we can only muster up enough energy to go through the motions of existence.

You're not suppose to love every teacher you had in life. Be realistic, pick out a few good teachers in your life and appreciate the good they have done for you.

1001 Affirmations

So what's new today. Bad old days; Children today are tyrants. They contradict their parents, gobble their food, and tyrannize their teachers. Socrates (470-399 BC)

When you teach you are always giving. Giving whatever information you have to in order to take the students from where they are now to where they should be in your field of expertise.

Half of life is trying to get what you'd like to get and the other half is to enjoy what you have.

Basic Communications: Trust, Excellence and Care. Lou Holtz

On teaching; Age gives more valued experiences.

The more you criticize the more you will be criticized at a later date.

You know you're getting old when the candles cost more than the cake. Bob Hope

You cannot antagonize and influence at the same time.

What you do speaks so loudly I can't hear what you're saying.

Belief; The future belongs to those who believe in the beauty of their dreams.

If I have everything to gain and nothing to lose by trying, I'll by all means try.

If it hadn't been for some teacher, you wouldn't be where you are today.

RESPECT A MAN OF PRAYER; Trust Thyself and put your trust in the Lord.

When you come to your 50th anniversary you thank God for allowing you to get under the bar of life's problems without getting into too much trouble.

Directions for life. Associate with the successful, prosperous and saintly people in your family and community and help the poor and downtrodden get on their feet.

Everyone has a moral code they live by.

Eat, run, stay fit and die anyway.

ANTI STRESS KIT: BANG HEAD HERE. ☒

Some people think when you're a Christian you are a perfect individual. No, rather it is a journey to perfecting your interrelationships with GOD and man.

We are the living Bible. The Bible is what you do after you have read the words. _____

Rules Of The World

1. The world is not fair.
2. Everybody has a boss.
3. Living involves hassle.
4. Nobody is entitled to anything.
5. True pride is self respect and must be earned not gifted.
6. Being loved is only for babies after that reciprocity is required.
7. Everybody goofs around a lot.
8. Everybody is laughable.
9. Staying busy is work.

Unknown

God grant me the serenity to accept the things I cannot change, courage to change the things I can and the wisdom to know the difference. Living one day at a time, enjoying one moment at a time; accepting hardship as the pathway to peace. Taking as He did this sinful world as it is, not as I would have it; trusting that He will make all things right if I surrender to His will; that I may be reasonably happy in this life; and supremely happy with Him forever in the next. Reinhold Niebuhr

Herbert P. Windschitl

Blessings

The man whispered, "God speak to me!" and the meadowlark sang. The man did not hear.

So the man yelled. "God, speak to me!" and the thunder rolled across the sky. But the man did not listen.

The man looked around and said. "God, let me see you." and a star shone brightly. But the man didn't notice.

And the man shouted. "God show me a miracle." and a life was born, but the man did not know.

So the man cried out in despair. "Touch me God and let me know you are here." Whereupon God reached down and touched the man. But the man brushed the butterfly away and walked on. Unknown.

Master Teacher

1. Caring, 2. Clarity, 3. Confidence, 4. Commitment, 5. Consistency, 6. Creativity. 7. What can I do to help you? 8. What can I get you to make the job easier? 9. Tell me what I can do and you've got it. 10. Insert "Take 10"into the lesson plans /End of class / Or reward.
Leadership Lane, Manhattan Kansas

No one is greater than his teacher until he becomes a teacher. The Gospel.

The World Is Full Of Goodness: 500,000 CATHOLIC MASSES are said every day, 21,000 every hour; 347 every minute; 6 each second.

The two great commandments are to Love God with your whole heart, your whole mind and love your neighbor as yourself. This in Benedictine terms is Worship and work. They've been around 1500 years.

Herbert P. Windschitl

A B C's of happiness. Valett

Aspire to reach your potential. Believe in yourself.
Create a good life. Dream about what you might become.
Exercise frequently.   Forgive honest mistakes.
Glorify the creative spirit.   Humor yourself and others.
Image great things.   Joyfully live each day.
Kindly help others.   Love one another. Meditate daily.
Nurture environment.   Organize for harmonious action.
Praise performance well done. Question most things.
Regulate you own behavior.   Smile often.   Think rationally. Understand yourself.   Value life.
Work for the common good.   X ray to carefully examine problem.   Yearn to improve. Zestfully pursue happiness.

Remember those who have no voices but who have needs. Nick Coleman

A Diplomat is a person who can tell you to go to hell in such a way that you actually look forward to the trip.

Your ignorance shows. Be careful when you open your mouth so as not to remove all doubt.

You are known by where you hang out. Is their anything wrong with hanging out in church?

Society comes together at times to do things that are right as a whole.

If you will only believe part of what you hear about me; I'll only believe half of what I hear about you.

All you have to do in order to have a better job is to do a better job.

Fatherhood starts in the love of a woman.

In marriage, as in all endeavors, we feel we deserve better.

Ignorance is voluntary misfortune. If you think education is expensive try ignorance.

Attitude is the mind's paintbrush. It can color any situation.

Today's activities will be tomorrow's memories.

There are no bad kids. Only bad ideas that make bad kids.

Every thing I needed to know about life was found in World Book.

The only people who don't buy books are the ones that know it all.

Lifetime goals. Jewish Rabbi. Plant a tree; raise a child; write a book.

It's not that life is so short but that you're dead so long.

The only people that don't need to go to the church are the one's that are perfect and they know it all. The rest of us are sinners and still learning about God's kingdom.

Be thankful for fools. Without them, the rest of us wouldn't look so good.

I've been retired for so long I can't remember what I did for a living.

A salesman's expression; There's nothing like a faithful wife, an old dog, and ready money.

Integrity is doing what's right and feeling good about yourself.

I wish I could come before the Lord and say I've never sinned, but all I can say is Lord have mercy on me a sinner.

You have to give a man a chance to be a rat before you can categorize him as one.

Marriage elopement; We all have some of the wild side in us, but in retrospect life would be a downer if we did not respect the sacred side of marriage and family.

If you're married; ACT like you're married.

I'm rich in spirit but not in money or material goods.

Did someone catch you praying today. Be on line with Prayer, Fasting and Almsgiving.

It's known that people who have close family ties and go to church regularly live longer than others do.

If you have nothing to do; Don't do it here! Life doesn't owe anyone a free ride.

There are no rules here—we're trying to accomplish something. Thomas Edison

I love deadlines. I like the whooshing sound they make as they fly by. Douglas Adams

God gave us two ends! One to sit on and one to think with. Success depends upon which one we use the most. Heads we win; tails we lose.

In Hannibal, Missouri when I was a boy, everybody was poor, but didn't know it, and everybody that was comfortable did know it. Mark Twain

Attitude is 10% what happens to me and 90% of how I react to what happens to me.

The Pen is mightier than the sword.

I'm not going to tell you what to do. You have to do what you feel is right and I have to do what I feel is right after you're done with your decision.

Herbert P. Windschitl

Be religious or be damned. St. John Vianney

It is fitting and proper to thank our parents for the gift of life. The Church does not say we have to believe in private miracles, but to those that believe no explanation is necessary and those that do not believe no explanation is possible.

You can't possibly give back to your parents what they have done for you. Just give them honest appreciation. They'll know what you mean.

In moving forward in our work we must have faith in things unseen and let it be known what we are doing.

The Bible states back to back 365 times the words FEAR NOT. Kinder

Think; Believe; See; Dare and then some. If it is to be; It's up to me. Kinder

The world becomes evil to a greater or lesser extent because of the times good men fail to say or do anything.

Do more than exist, LIVE; Do more than touch, FEEL; Do more than look, OBSERVE; Do more than read, ABSORB; Do more than hear, LISTEN; Do more than listen, UNDERSTAND; Do more than think, PONDER; Do more than talk, SAY SOMETHING. John Rhodes

Dreams

Hold fast to dreams; For if dreams die; Life is a broken winged bird; That cannot fly. Hold fast to dreams. For when dreams go; Life is a barren field; Frozen with snow. Langston Hughes.

Good people do bad things. This is not good but this just happens.

Letting Go

Today I will open myself to the love that is coming to me from the universe. I do not push or struggle for greater acceptance. This moment I am free to express myself in love, joy and enthusiasm.

I believe in my religion; I believe in myself; I believe in my products; I believe in my work; I believe in my company; I believe I am going to have a good day.

Herbert P. Windschitl

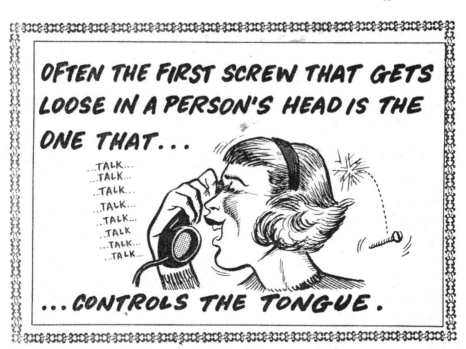

Herbert P. Windschitl

A B C's Of Selling. Always Be Closing.

Books make the world go around and we need strong motivational ideas to use them for our self improvement.

Above all be honest with yourself. As Emerson once said, we need to "Vibrate to that iron string of life."

A child's mind will not fail you if you do not fail it.

Right angle thought. I understand we all must die some day but I don't want to be present when it happens to me. Woody Allen

First we make our habits and then our habits make us or break us.

No one can make you feel inferior without your consent. Eleanor Roosevelt

Do the thing you fear the most and the death of fear is certain. Emerson

Don't wear you heart on your shirt sleeve where others can put you down.

To be informed is to be protected.

Power is overwhelming someone. Authority is what remains after the conflict.

Failure is a part of the infinite plan. Who finds he can't must give away to who can, and as each and another drop out of the race, he stumbleth at last to his suitable place. Owen Meredith

The message is right, but the messenger is wrong.

I want to talk to the organ grinder rather than who's at the end of the leash.

I was called to serve not to succeed in life. We can't help everyone on the streets. Mother Teresa

God will provide and with my help I will survive.

Eye contact is OK but be aware of the controlling factors when people force eye contact on you. Direct eye contact is asking for complete submission to his or her ideas. Suddenly you find yourself in an irreversible mode of thinking.

Jack Morris, Game 7 of the world series said, "I care, I guess that's the bottom line. I've made a lot of mistakes, but I keep trying to do better. I guess that's what you're suppose to do in this crazy world we live in."

Four Wants In Life: 1. Want to live, 2. Prestige—Power—Recognition, 3. Money, 4. New different things. What do you want? Insanity is not inherited—people want it.

Time Management: 1. Personal, 2. Profit, 3. Potential. Four functions of management are: 1. Planning, 2. Organizing, 3. Motivating, 4. Controlling or evaluating.

Basic Needs: 1. Physical, 2. Safety or security needs, 3. Social or love needs, 4. Self actualization or self fulfillment needs. Will to meaning in life.

Success Essentials: 1. Set goals, 2. Develop written plans and deadlines, 3. Burning desire, 4. Supreme confidence, 5. Iron willed determination.

Goals Must Be: 1. Personal in nature, 2. Stated positively, 3. Realistic and attainable, 4. Includes some personality changes.

I want not only effort but results.

Keep moving to do something to reach your goals.

Just because the bird of trouble flies over your head, we don't have to let him build a nest in our hair. Chinese proverb.

Trouble comes to pass, not to stay.

Warriors Cry: "Lead, follow or get the hell out of the way."

Formula For Handling People: 1. Listen to the other person's story, 2. Listen to the other person's full story, 3. Listen to the other person's full story first. Gen G. Marshall

Remember the road you travel.

The only people who never fail—are those who never try. Erma Bombeck

You've worked but what have you gotten out of it.

Readers are leaders.

When you get a lemon in life, make lemonade.

Every day in every way I'm getting better and better.

Are you a problem preventor or a problem solver? Are you a part of the problem and a part of the solution?

Thieves Of Time: 1. Procrastination, 2. Excuses, 3. Regrets.

Develop a consistent plan of work. Keep a time schedule of activity in writing.

Help a man to fish and he will starve not a day. Teach a man how to fish and he will starve not a lifetime. Chinese proverb.

Why settle for less when you can have the best.

In sales the element of surprise is worth a pound of gold.

Army Engineers Motto: We do the most difficult task first. The impossible takes a little longer.

Isn't quality remembered a long time after the price is forgotten?

Just suppose it does what you'd like it to do, would you want it?

People like to be bothered with new ideas and concepts.

Be gracious with people but stubborn with time.

An order in the hand is worth two in the bush.

Do everything right everytime in every way no matter how you feel.

Keep alive a little story or joke every day.

Selling is teaching: Find out what the other person wants and then help him get it.

Slow down when you have a fearful situation. Talk slower instead of faster.

Picture yourself already in possession of your goal. This is not Pollyanna thinking. We feel good about ourselves or we feel bad about ourselves. Think what you will.

Sales Strategy, CC—CD—CC Create Confidence: Create desire, Close collect and go get the next one.

ABA Always Be Asking: Develop a consistent plan of action.

Major move toward success: 1. Work, 2. Preparation, 3. Purpose. Study revealed 35% unwilling to work; 22% Lack of preparation and taking suggestions; 20% Lack of purpose and resolve.

Books make the world go around if we only let them influence us.

First you make your habits then your habits make you.

If there's anything definite in life it's CHANGE.

The best way to sell—Make it convenient to buy.

Sometimes when life hands us a lemon we're miserable and we don't even know it.

It's a known fact that a pregnant woman will give birth to a baby that needs at least 18 years of special love that only a mother & father can give. Are you ready for the challenge? Be careful of who you share your deepest feelings with for they will come true.

Old nursery rhyme. Sticks and stones may break my bones but words will never hurt you. We all know words can hurt you.

Herbert P. Windschitl

Life's Activities To Keep Us Active

1. Say a prayer.
2. Do a good deed.
3. Give a drink of water to someone.
4. Read the new testament.
5. Read the old testament.
6. Get to know Jesus for eternal life.
7. Right a wrong done to a friend.
8. Hug a spouse or friend.
9. Hug a child.
10. Read the 10 commandments.
11. Read the beatitudes.
12. Tell someone about a good teacher you had.
13. Forgive yourself.
14. Do God's will in your life.
15. Keep an upper lip when trouble comes.
16. Feed the hungry. Make a home meal.
17. Do some charity.
18. Go to Mass on Sunday.
19. Write a letter.
20. Do something toward your personal goals.
21. Set a goal.
22. Find ways to love your work, and keep moving on.
23. Eat sensibly.
24. Worship and work is a good motto.
25. Read the life of a saint.
26. Say an act of contrition.
27. Read the precepts of the church.
28. Visit the sick.
29. Counsel the doubtful.

30. Comfort the sorrowful.
31. Bear wrongs patiently.
32. Pray for the living and dead.
33. Educate yourself to face life's challenges.
34. Read a magazine.
35. Develop a healthy fear and love of the Lord.
36. Do some traveling.
37. Always promote faith, hope and charity.
38. Be prudent.
39. Promote justice.
40. Study your religion.
41. Be strong in the face of challenges.
42. Tell someone you love them.
43. Accept anothers love and concern for you.
44. Look up to people, never down to them.
45. Cope with stress in a positive way.
46. Exercise.
47. When you do something good, be proud to say I'm glad I did it.
48. Take pride in your elders because they're proud of you.
49. Concentrate on one task at a time.
50. Smile at people.
51. Do a favor for someone even if you don't like them.
52. Mind your own business.
53. Make a duplicate of all your keys.
54. Plant a tree, a garden or mow the grass.
55. Play a game of cards.
56. Play a game of checkers or chess.
57. Take out the garbage.
58. Pull a weed.
59. Watch a sunset.
60. Watch it rain.

61. Go to a good play.
62. See a good movie.
63. Get out and vote.
64. Share an apple slice with a friend.
65. Get up extra early to experience the morning.
66. Send a card.
67. Give a gift.
68. Go to confession to feel God's mercy.
69. Forgive a transgression.
70. Read a motivational book.
71. Listen to a good speaker.
72. Listen to your favorite music.
73. Be positive about life, it's God's gift to you.
74. Gradually put away the things of a child.
75. Be a man.
76. Be a woman.
77. Enjoy your life.
78. Grow old with dignity.
79. Be slow to criticize.
80. Win the friendship of a difficult person.
81. Hate evil.
82. Always love the person even if he wrongs you.
83. Drive carefully because your life depends on it.
84. Respect your life and others.
85. Keep interested in your career no matter how trivial it is.
86. Be a homemaker not a home wrecker.
87. Be kind to your enemies, after all, you made them.
88. Help a neighbor.
89. Rise and shine in the morning.
90. Be out front leading or get out of the way and follow.
91. Be on guard. The world is full of trickery and deceit.

92. Repeat to yourself a favorite song and poem.
93. Be an active member in your church.
94. Be a friend in order to get a friend.
95. Jesus promotes the Power of Love not the love of power.
96. If God is for us who can be against us.
97. Seek first the kingdom of God and all other things will be added unto you.
98. Rejoice and be glad—This is the day the Lord has made.
99. God loves a cheerful giver.
100. Moving out of fixed positions is the mark of a holy person. Once we no longer move out of fixed positions we become finished. We end our humanity and quest of God.

Herbert P. Windschitl

Teacher Motivation
Start the day with these words

I feel like a great teacher. No one has a greater right to teach these students then I. I have been hired by someone whom the community respects.

I will use controlled attention, concentrated energy, and sustained effort to teach these students. I have empathy for them, compassion for them and I care for each student as a human being created by God with certain rights and responsibilities.

I can see through the students eyes the end results they will gain from my teaching here. I will enter this classroom situation without giving mental recognition to the possibility of defeat.

I will allow no student to keep me from teaching here. I will allow no student to keep another from learning in my classroom. When I'm teaching, I know, the students know, when I mean business.

I will do everything right every time in every way no matter how I feel. My students benefit from my teaching more and more each day I am here.

The EDUCATIONAL PROCESS: The teachers and administrators along with the cooperation of the youth, parents and board of education run the school for the benefit and education of each student.

BETWEEN TEACHER AND CHILD. I have come to the frightening conclusion I am the decisive element in the classroom. It is my personal approach that creates the climate. It is my daily mood that makes the weather. As a teacher I possess tremendous power to make a child's life miserable or joyous. I can be tool of torture or an instrument of inspiration. I can humiliate or humor; hurt or heal. In all situations it is my response that decides whether a crisis will be escalated or deescalated, and a child humanized or dehumanized. Dr. Hiram Ginott

What's behind this classroom door I do not know, but this I know the more I open the more I'll teach. If I have everything to gain and nothing to lose by trying, I'll by all means try.

I'LL DO IT NOW

Driving Is A Privilege Not A Right: Be Alert. Drive carefully. Keep a good air cushion between cars. Always drive according to road conditions.

Conscientious Behavior: Your behavior is seen by others, so watch yourself. Others know you and they also tell stories. That's your reward or punishment. When you open your mouth your mind is on parade.

On my honor I will do my best. To do my duty to God and my country. To keep myself physically fit mentally awake and morally strait. Boy Scout oath.

It's not true you're stupid if you don't know everything. It's sufficient to be interested. Wally Cox

We all want to live a life that matters for significance in this world, a belief that we're a good person, noticed and recognized.

In some way God lets you know when your true love comes along in life.

Love is not love which alters when alterations find. Shakespeare

I've made up my mind, don't confuse me with the facts.

Aren't we hypocrites when we want to get to heaven but don't do anything to favor God and His Church, in this physical world?

I will admit my faith in the Lord is stronger than my intelligence.

Look at Moses. He was educated by the Egyptians during his youthful days. As an adult he led the people of Israel to freedom and suffered greatly to get the Ten Commandments from God.

No man on his death bed has said, I didn't spend enough time with my business.

We must all be answerable to God for what we do. God bless our words and actions each day, for they do influence others.

I'm trying to tell parents right is right and wrong is wrong. But some parents tell me wrong is right.

I owe, I owe; To work to work I go.

Put your faith and hope in educated people; Education is man's gift to man. Faith in the gospels is God's gift to man.

Children like to be led into fine books. Buy them the best.

Kids street crossing. Look to the left, look to the right; before you cross the street. First you use your eyes; then you use your ears; before you use your feet.

"Living well is the best revenge." Alex Korda

If it's real love it'll return to you. If it doesn't come back, it isn't real love.

The hardest thing to do in marriage is to forgive and forget, and then to move on to new experiences.

I can live on one nice compliment for 3 months.

Marriage doesn't begin until you're about ready to kick him or her out. You then realize I've married my partner for life and this is just a road block to a loving relationship.

Herbert P. Windschitl

Twenty two suggestions for success

1. Marry the right person. The one decision will determine 90% of your happiness or misery. 2. Work on something you enjoy that's worth your time & talent. 3. Give people more than you expect and do it cheerfully. 4. Become the most positive and enthusiastic person you know. 5. Be forgiving of yourself and others. 6. Be generous. 7. Have a grateful heart. 8. Have persistence, persistence and persistence. 9. Discipline yourself to save money on even the most modest salary. 10. Trust everyone you meet like you want to be trusted. 11. Commit yourself to constant improvement. 12. Commit yourself to Quality. 13. Under-stand happiness is not based on possessions, power, prestige, but on relationships with people you love and respect. 14. Be Loyal. 15. Be Honest. 16. Be a self starter. 17. Be decisive even if it means being wrong sometimes. 18. Stop blaming others. 19. Take responsibility of every area of your life. 20. Be bold and courageous. When you look back on your life you'll regret the things you didn't do more than the things you did. 21. Take care of those you love. 22. Don't do anything that wouldn't make your Mom proud.
    H. Jackson Brown Jr.

We must all be answerable to God for what we do. God bless our words and actions each day, for they do influence others.

FOUR LAST THINGS

Death, Judgement, Heaven or Hell.

Gaelic Blessing

"May the road rise to meet you,
May the wind always be at your back,
May the sun shine upon your face,
And the rains fall softly upon your fields,
And, until we meet again,
May God hold you in the palm of His hand.

The Scout Oath

On my honor, I will do my best—To do my duty to God and my Country, and to obey the Scout Law; To help other people at all times; To keep myself physically strong, mentally awake and morally straight.

The Scout Law

A Scout is: Trustworthy, Loyal, Helpful, Friendly, Courteous, Kind, Obedient, Cheerful, Thrifty, Brave, Clean and Reverent.

Herbert P. Windschitl

___Sales Motivation___

I am a great sales person. No one has a greater right to call on this prospect than I. I have been sent to see this prospect by someone he respects.

I will use controlled attention, concentrated energy, and sustained effort. I have empathy and compassion for my prospect, and I care for him as a human being.

I can see the end result benefits which I know this prospect will experience from using the program.

I will enter this sales situation without giving mental recognition to the possibility of defeat.

What's behind the door I do not know.
But this I know and know it well.
The more I open the more I sell.

If I have everything to gain and nothing to lose by trying, I'll by all means try.

I'll DO IT NOW

MY GOALS FOR: _____ _____
1. _____
2. _____
3. _____
4. _____
5. _____
6. _____
7. _____
8. _____
9. _____
10. _____

Make 5 demonstrations 45 minutes long with 5 closes each; Results 1 sale. Make 25. Go for it!

High sentiments always win in the end. The leaders who offer blood, toil, tears and sweat, always get more out of their followers than those who offer safety and a good time. When it comes to the pinch, human beings are heroic. George Orwell

I play to win. I plan to win. I think like a winner. I act like a winner. I share my victories.

The road to success is marked with tempting parking spaces.

Learn like you're going to live forever. Live like you're going to die tomorrow.

When you try to change another person you're in trouble.

When you help another person get what he wants you're a friend.

Faust—new coach at Notre Dame—You better not cuss. You better not play dirty football. And if you burp, you better say "Excuse me." JMJ

Above all, service to others is my lot in life.

Worry robs your life of strength rather than emptying your problems.

David slew Goliath. He didn't think about Goliath or the hugh obstacle so much as he thought about his dream of a woman and freeing his people. Focus on dreams. What are your Goliath's in life?

He is my enemy. I am not his enemy. Can we recognize our friends among our enemies. It's just as important to see our negative influences as well as our positive influences.

Lord, what will you have me do? Acts 9:6 Always do one task at a time.

Friendship doubles our joy and divides our grief.

Follow through with your word. When I was young, anytime I accepted a task, it was considered done.

In some situations you have to be mean in order to do good. The Lord came to promote division, not peace in the sense of the world's thinking.

Sitting there wishing makes no person great. The good Lord sends us fishing. You must dig the bait.

What does the Lord require of you? To do justice, to love mercy, and to walk humbly with God. Micah 6:8.

I love leaders that point the direction. I hate bosses.

None of us is as smart as all of us.

Be careful how you live, you may be the only Bible some person reads.

Don't be afraid to give your best to what seemingly are small jobs. Every time you conquer one it makes you that much stronger. If you do the little jobs well, the big ones will tend to take care of themselves. Dale Carnegie

If a man does not keep pace with his companions, perhaps it is because he hears a different drummer. Let him step to the music which he hears, however measured or far away. Thoreau

Many quarreled about religion that never practiced it.

Be eternally discontent with the status quo. Dr. Nault

Herbert P. Windschitl

If you think something can go wrong, it will go wrong. Murphy's law

"Love in practice is a harsh and dreadful thing compared to love in dreams." Brothers Karamozov

Let us go forth, to lead the land we love knowing that His work, must truly be our own. JFK.

Total power is a dangerous thing. Dominating other people destroys justice.

A PRAYER

AND THOU SHALT CALL HIS NAME JESUS.
PRINCE OF PEACE, MIGHTY GOD,
WONDERFUL COUNSELOR, HOLY ONE,
LAMB OF GOD, PRINCE OF LIFE, LORD
GOD ALMIGHTY
LION OF THE TRIDE OF JUDA. ROOT OF DAVID,
WORD OF LIFE, AUTHOR AND FINISHER OF OUR
FAITH. ADVOCATE, THE WAY, DAY SPRING,
LORD OF ALL, I AM, SON OF GOD, SHEPHERD AND
BISHOP OF SOULS. MESSIAH, TRUTH, SAVIOR.
CHIEF CORNERSTONE, KING OF KINGS,
RIGHTEOUS JUDGE, LIGHT OF THE WORLD.
HEAD OF THE CHURCH, MORNING STAR,
SON OF THE RIGHTEOUS, LORD JESUS CHRIST,
CHIEF SHEPHERD. RESURRECTION AND LIFE.
HORN OF SALVATION, GOVERNOR,
THE ALPHA AND OMEGA.

Herbert P. Windschitl

Happiness in life is in the beatitudes

Sermon on the Mount

1. Blessed are the poor in spirit, for theirs is the kingdom of heaven.
2. Blessed are the meek, for they shall possess the earth.
3. Blessed are they who mourn for they shall be comforted.
4. Blessed are they who hunger and thirst for justice, for they shall be satisfied.
5. Blessed are the merciful, for they shall obtain mercy.
6. Blessed the pure of heart, for they shall see God.
7. Blessed are the peacemakers, for they shall be called the children of God.
8. Blessed are they who suffer persecution for justice' sake for theirs is the kingdom of heaven.
9. Blessed are you when men revile you and persecute you and utter all kinds of evil against you falsely on my account. Rejoice and be glad, for your reward is great in heaven. Matthew 5:3–12

The duties toward God and neighbor

The Ten Commandments of God

1. I am the Lord thy God. Thou shalt not have strange gods before me.
2. Thou shalt not take the name of the Lord thy God in vain.
3. Remember thou keep holy the Sabbath day.
4. Honor thy father and thy mother.
5. Thou shalt not kill.
6. Thou shalt not commit adultery.
7. Thou shalt not steal.
8. Thou shalt not bear false witness against thy neighbor.
9. Thou shalt not covet thy neighbor's wife.
10. Thou shalt not covet thy neighbor's goods.

The duties toward the church

1. To assist at Mass on Sundays and holy days of obligations.
2. To fast and abstain on certain days.
3. To receive Holy communion during the Easter season.
4. To confess our sins once a year.
5. To contribute what is necessary for divine worship, for the maintenance of the church.
6. To observe the church's regulations on marriage.

Herbert P. Windschitl

Nicene Creed

Man cannot be perfectly happy in this world, for nothing created can satisfy his desire for complete happiness. History and experience show that neither riches, nor honors, nor glory, nor reputation, nor power, nor pleasure, nor knowledge, nor any other worldly goods can fully satisfy man's longing for happiness. Man's earthly imperfect happiness is in proportion to his approach to God. The final goal of his life.
Anonymous

Meditations of Faith

Meditations for the busy man or woman that can be repeated many times while on the go in this busy world in which we live. Simplicity and Silence. Add some of your own favorites.

Seven little words

"Let thirst and fasting be our share."
"Do not be afraid, just have faith."
"Unclean spirit come out of the man."
"Who do people say that I am?"
"Little girl, I say to you arise!"
"I am the resurrection and the life."

Five little words

"How do I love thee?"
"Let me count the ways." Browning
"Your faith has healed you."
"Rise and have no fear."
"Who hath done this deed?" Emilia, Othello
"Light shines in the darkness."
"I will be with you." Moses and burning bush
"Make haste to help me."
"Go and sin no more."
"I believe help my unbelief."
"Jesus said to her, Mary."
"Sit here while I pray."
"I will send an angel."
"My Lord and my God."
"Serve the Lord with gladness."
"Love is strong as death."
"And they all forsook him."

Herbert P. Windschitl

"Why hast thou forsaken Me?"
"You will be like God." Serpent to Eve
"Say you are my sister." Abraham's least golden moment said to Sarah as the Egyptians looked on.

Four little words

"All shall be well." Mother Julian "Get behind me Satan."
"Do you love me?" Jesus to Peter 3 times
"What is your name?"

Three little words

"So Abram went."
"He is Risen."
"Go in peace."
"Quiet! Be still."
"You say so."
"Watch and Pray."

Two little words

Stand fast. (Lonely Abbey.)
"Jesus wept."
"Yes Lord."
"He prayed."
"He fasted."
"Pray always."
"Be open."
"Follow me."

One little word

"AMEN."
"Alleluia."
"Watch."
"Pray."

1001 Affirmations

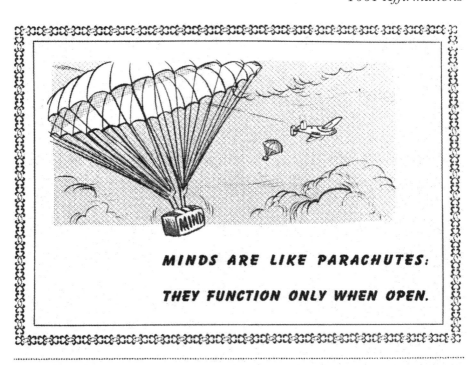

MINDS ARE LIKE PARACHUTES:
THEY FUNCTION ONLY WHEN OPEN.

DEFINITION OF <u>OPPORTUNITY</u>:
SOMETHING OFTEN MISSED BECAUSE
WE ARE BROADCASTING WHEN WE
SHOULD BE TUNING IN.

Herbert P. Windschitl

A GOOD PERSON HAS NO WAY OF PROVING IT

... EXCEPT BY WHAT HE DOES.

ANYWAY, HEAVY RESPONSIBILITIES ON YOUR SHOULDERS DO HELP TO KEEP YOUR FEET ON THE GROUND!

Ten Rules Of Success

1. Find your talent.
2. Be big.
3. Be honest.
4. Live with enthusiasm.
5. Don't let your possession possess you.
6. Don't worry about your problems.
7. Look up to people when you can. Down to no one.
8. Don't cling to the past.
9. Assume your share of responsibility in the world.
10. PRAY consistently and confidently.
Unknown

Interrelationships are most important.

Don't solve problems but pursue opportunities.

It all boils down to Love & Truth. Gandhi

Evils: The World, The Flesh and The Devil.

Riches evils are Injustice and preoccupation.

The strong are ask to help the weak.

What do you mean you're over the hill. You've never been to the top.

Herbert P. Windschitl

It doesn't really make any difference where you came from but where do you want to go.

It's more important to know how to grow old then it is to be a child.

When you wish you had your old job back—that means you've hit bottom.

He who's not busy being born is busy dying. B. Dylan

Lord bless this bunch as we munch our lunch.

Services here: Answers $.75; Answers requiring thought. $1.25; Correct answers $2.50; Dumb looks Free.

In marriage you need to expect a few things from each other, but be careful that you do not demand an entire support system from the other spouse.

There is an imaginary line between husband and wife relationships. If someone violates that trust, distrust and anger sets in.

Either we stand up for peace or we find ourselves in the middle of war.

The secret of success is to set aside 8 hours a day for work and 8 hours for sleep. Make sure they're not the same 8 hours.

Build on your strengths and never compare your weaknesses to other's strengths. Bart Breighner

Caution: Under the influence of children.

Slogans on stress: "Easy does it." "One day at a time." "First things first."

The complete victory is to triumph over oneself. <u>Imitation of Christ</u> Thomas Kempis 1440.

An estate auction is a fast and efficient way to move your belongings into the hands of needy neighbors.

Mark Twain was once asked why he hadn't gone to the funeral of a widely known leader in the community. Twain quipped back that he knew the man.

You can be a good person without going to church but you can't be a good Christian without going to church.

Struggling is beautiful: The struggles we have in life make us strong and beautiful. Without the cross we would be nothing but a vegetable without life. Everyone has different struggles. Find yours and make it a tree upon which you can lean on.

Create a problem and then offer a solution. Most people want to find a solution to a problem.

We give away our power when we think we have none.

I think that I shall never see the dollar that I loaned to thee;
A dollar that I could have spent on many forms of merriment.
The one I loaned to you so gladly; is now the one I need so badly.
For whose return I had great hope; just like an optimistic dope.
For dollars loaned to folks like thee; are not returned to fools like me. Ann Landers

Desire To Grow: 1. Positive Mind, 2. Goals, 3. Self Image, 4. Mind set.

Learn To Be Passionately Against Something: Dirt vs cleanliness; Ignorance vs knowledge; Hate vs love; Evil vs good; Laziness vs energetic; Doubt vs faith; Sin vs grace; Devil vs God. We are what we think about all day long.

Love is something you do, not always something you can feel, but it's real. Love is something you do when Jesus Christ is living in you.

You can get through school without going to church but it's almost impossible to get to heaven without going to church.

Man's greatest sin is man's inhumanity to man.

Here I am, Father, show me your authority.
Here I am, Lord, show me your love.
Here I am, Holy Spirit, teach me your ways and speak to me.

Five stages in dying: 1. Denial; 2. Anger; 3. Bargaining; 4. Depression; 5. Acceptance.

Because I could not stop for death; It stopped for me. Emily Dickinson

Time wasted can never be returned.

Anyone that doesn't buy good books for their children is an animal. State Fair. 1981 former book customer.

Notice: While in this office speak in a low and soothing tone and do not disagree with me in any manner. Please be informed that when one has reached my age, noise and non concurrence cause gastric hyperperistatsis; hypersecretion; of the hydrocholic acid, and rubus of gastric naucosa—and I may become most unpleasant!!!

Relish the moment: Psalm 118:24. THIS IS THE DAY THE LORD HAS MADE; LET US BE GLAD AND REJOICE IN IT. It isn't the burden of today that drives men mad. It is regret of yesterday and fear of tomorrow. Regret and fear are twin thieves who rob us today. Life must be lived as we go along. Thinking like when I'm 18; when I have a Mercedes; or when my last kid is through college etc; holds you back.

Positive Mental Attitude

Monday is good; Tuesday is great; Wednesday is fantastic; Thursday is marvelous; Friday is super; Saturday is stupendous; Sunday is grand. There is no such thing as a bad day. Only some are better than others.

Herbert P. Windschitl

Plan your work and work your plan. Keep moving doing something toward your goals. Don't let a job interfere with your life and don't let the school interfere with your education.

We need to live our lives with a high profile or a low profile. God needs us both.

Herbert P. Windschitl

Am I a Builder?

I watched them tearing a building down.
A gang of men in a busy town.
With a ho heave ho and a lusty yell
They swung a beam, and the sidewall fell,
I asked the foreman, "Are these men skilled.
Are they men you'd hire if you had to build?"
He laughed and said; "No, indeed!
Just common labor is all I need.
I can easily wreck in a day or two
What builders have taken a year to do."

And I thought to myself as I went away,
Which of these roles do I try to play?
Am I a builder who works with care,
Measuring life by the rule and the square?
Am I shaping my deeds to a well made plan
Patiently doing the best I can?
Or am I a wrecker who walks the town
Content with the labor of tearing down?
AUTHOR UNKNOWN

To be nobody but myself in a world which is doing its best, night and day, to make you everybody else—means to fight the hardest battle which any human being can fight, and never stop fighting. e e commings

Herbert P. Windschitl

I don't know where I'm going, but I'm on my way.

It's difficult to soar with eagles when you work with turkeys.

Work, Loyalty and Love are prime prerequisites. Vince Lombardi

We must learn about the past in History in order to help us to live in the future.

We need schools that turn out students that are still willing to learn.

Spend more time on interpersonal relationships, rather than on material benefits in life. Dr. Hunt. On Dying.

The eagle gets its prey by one in three attempts.

Happiness

Is anybody happier because you passed his way?
Does anyone remember that you spoke to him today?
The day is almost over, and its toiling time is through;
Is there anyone to utter now a kindly word of you?
Can you say tonight, in parting with the day that's slipping fast,
That you helped a single brother of the many that you passed?
Is a single heart rejoicing over what you did or said;
Does the man whose hopes were fading, now with courage look ahead?
Did you waste the day, or lose it; was it well or sorely spent?
Did you leave a trail of kindness, or a scar of discontent?
As you close your eyes in slumber, do you think that God will say,
You have earned one more tomorrow by the work you did today?
Anonymous

Don't keep these a secret. Tell others: 1. I like my work, 2. I make mistakes, 3. I like you, 4. I feel lousy sometimes, 5. I have a pet peeve, 6. It doesn't make any difference to me, 7. I'm basically happy, 8. I believe in God.

Some public opinion often says we should not force our Christian concepts of right and wrong on others; yet this same public opinion will force secular humanism and worldly success upon us with the zeal of a crusader.

St. Alphonus Ligiuori writes; If you pray you are positive of saving your soul. If you do not pray you are just as positive of losing your soul.

How To Stay Married

Couples who are married in Church and continue to regularly attend church do not have a 1 in 3 divorce rate. Instead, only 1 in 50 of their marriages end in divorce. And among couples who marry in church, continue to attend church, and also have a prayer life at home, only 1 in 1105 of these get divorced. These figures do not come from some church survey. They have been gleaned from the 1980 US Census report.

Your own personal goals and purpose are more important than any of the loftiest ideas.

Organizations and businesses need your hands and feet to make them successful. Christ also needs your hands and feet to make His love known throughout the world.

You can stay out as late as you want as long as you get up at 6 AM.

What goes around comes around.

We get along real well in our family; We live far enough apart.

Success is a journey not a destination.

Women love about husbands. Love; Sensitivity; Way with children; Looks; Money; Sexual prowess.

Are we in tune with life or in tune with business.

Home making can be a career in itself.

70% of the families in the top 5% had encyclopedias before the age of 4.

Give the lady what she wants. The customer is always right. Nault 1984

He's got a clean mind because he changes it so often.

Good answers and questions make the world go around.

You live by the gun, you die by the gun. You live by the bottle, you die by the bottle.

Over the years I've learned that the best thing to do is never touch a kid unless you put your arm around him and say you're doing great kid.

If we pitched as hard when we're not in trouble as we pitch to get out of trouble, we wouldn't get in trouble in the the first place. Casey Stengel

Don't feel entirely responsible for what happens in married life, you'll always find that part of your married life has slipped away. Learn to move to new experiences and learn from mistakes.

You can't fire me! Slaves have to be sold.

Try to relive your achievements and successes; NOT your failures and struggles.

I can get along with him, but it just seems he can't get along with me.

My minds awhirl. My body aches. I'm all worn out from coffee breaks.

If you knock part of what is said you make the other person human. If you knock everything the other person said you make yourself an idiot.

Order Of Our Personal Work Is: Individualism, Partnership or Business. Learn to live your own life.

Learning how to learn is sometimes more important than learning some facts.

Don't envy a good salesperson; Be one. Take your frustrations out by doing a better job.

In sales we sometimes become a professional failure; We fail more times than we succeed; But keep on trying.

I don't want to put words in your mouth because it's unsanitary.

When you fall off the horse, get up and try again or you may never try again. When you fail at a task, try and try again.

People aren't showing you a personal rejection but a misinformed judgment.

You don't own us. Only God can claim us. Educated people are difficult to drive but easy to lead.

Learning to live is more important than learning how to make money. Nevertheless making money also gives us opportunities to do the things we want to do.

A fool and his money are soon parted. Well how did they get together in the first place?

My parents had a crazy relationship; so when I wanted to come home too often, I decided not to; so that kept me on the job.

My wife beats me up every morning. I get up 15 minutes later.

Criteria For A Just War: 1. Just cause, 2. Competent authority, 3. Comparative justice, 4. Right intention, 5. Last resort, 6. Probability of success, 7. Proportionality of costs and damage. Minneapolis Tribune 1983 Bishops teaching.

Evangelization is like when I go to heaven I want to take some other people with me.

Herbert P. Windschitl

As long as I frequent the place of God I will not be very far off the track.

Confirmation is a matter of choosing good over evil. We commit ourselves to the best in life with the help of Jesus Christ.

Catholic schools sometimes picture Jesus as a young and youthful person full of fun and interested in games. He was this in reality up to age 30. Children don't always understand what real sacrifice is about.

We have met the enemy and it is us.

Not to decide is to decide.

The only dumb question is the one not asked.

It isn't that I'm a fast talker but that I talk fast.

A winner never quits while a quitter never wins.

Saint Joseph: A person working with his hands is always a free person in his own mind. This is true in relationship to any other occupation.

It takes 35 million laws to support the Ten Commandments.

There are two ways of spreading the light. To be the candle or the mirror that reflects it.

The Twelve Most Persuasive Words: Save, money, you, new, health, results, easy, safety, love, discovery, proven, guarantee.

There is nothing the matter with being poor but there is something the matter when you're ashamed to be poor.

Nothing happens until someone sells something.

We don't cash any checks here; we have enough left over from last year.

Only Robinson Crusoe could get everything done by Friday.

Beware of some little expenses. A little leak can sink a ship.

Be more concerned about what you think about others rather than about what others think about you.

Herbert P. Windschitl

Point of View

When the other fellow takes a long time, he's slow. When I take a long time, I'm thorough. When the other fellow doesn't do it, he's lazy. But when I don't do it, I'm busy. When the other fellow does something without being told, he's overstepping his bounds. But when I do it, that's initiative! When the other fellow takes a stand, he's bullheaded. But when I do it, I'm being firm. When the other fellow overlooks a rule of etiquette, he's rude. But when I skip a few rules, I'm original. When the other fellow pleases the boss, he's an apple polisher. But when I please the boss, that's co-operation. When the other fellow gets ahead, he's getting the breaks. But when I manage to get ahead, that's just the reward for hard work.
Anonymous

Sin has its penalties. Good works have their rewards.

I know enough to leave the boss do his job so I can do my job.

Life is meant to be lived. We must do something with our lives. Let's get on with living it. Regrets, procrastination, and excuses hold us back.

You can tell a man's character by what he pushes.

Marriage is like a one lane street. Make sure you're both going the same direction.

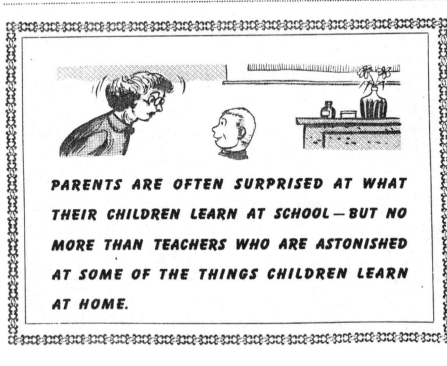

Don't cast your pearls to swine. Jesus

I am not afraid of tomorrow; For I have seen yesterday; And I love today.

Seek first the kingdom of God and all other things will be added unto you. Jesus.

We must learn to be reasonably dependent or we're doomed to be independent.

Confession is good for the soul. There is no salvation outside of the church.

Joy is not the absence of suffering, but the presence of God.

If you don't go to church, are you sure you can stand the heat.

Do not pray for easy lives. Pray to be a stronger person. Do not pray for tasks equal to your powers but pray for powers equal to your tasks.

Sex is for babies and then some.

God weeds out the weak through pain and struggle. The strong remain loyal to the Lord's teachings.

Take advantage of spiritual experience as well as other things in life. Some say Christianity has failed but I say Christianity hasn't been really tried.

When you're old enough and confident enough to get up and go, then get up and go.

Life does not stand still, even if we do. It moves on to make room for new experiences.

God's covenant: I am your God and you are my people.

When your son goes to college he'll be thankful for the time you invested in his future.

Everyone wants to get to heaven, but most people don't like how God expects us to get there.

When you have to ask someone whether you should get married or not, then you're not ready to get married.

We would like to live our lives as our forefathers did, but history won't let us. JFK Dallas

What we as a family mean to each other is worth more than any material gift.

Knowing how to get hired on a job and fired on a job and getting back on your feet is one of the most valuable experiences we can undergo in life.

Know Your Strengths And Limitations: Earnings capability, Health, Sports, Education, Family, Church and Friends.

Good feelings come from hard work; Good feelings that come easy are generally wrong; Good feelings about relationships takes hard work.

Which is more important money or knowledge? 1110 students polled said knowledge was the most important. 856 chose knowledge. Minneapolis Tribune 1983.

In all cases God is not all powerful; He weeps with you at this moment. He sent His son Jesus to show us the way the truth and the life; Death comes through nature.

My mother and father had a beef and stew relationship. She was always beefing and he was always stewed.

Theory of Divide and Conquer
With people—People win out.
With issues—Get your point across.
With ideas—compare and contrast; single out your ideas.
With things—offer other things in comparison to your ideas.

People buy on benefits, not necessarily the best; Emotion not logic; Want, not need. Continue to assume the sale or leave.

You don't have to pull as hard as you think to make a sale.

There are times when our lives seem to be falling apart around us, as did happen with the prophets in the Bible. But, we do not allow ourselves to fall apart. We are the temple of the Holy Spirit within us.

The more suffering, pain, problems and poor you are, the more God is with you. The rich, affluent, no problems, perfect health may be further from God than anyone else in this world. Our direction in life is to get closer to God. God is with the poor and suffering if we only look for Him.

The cross: The vertical is between God and man. The horizontal is our relationship to others.

Isn't it interesting; A teacher makes money because of ignorance; A farmer makes money because of hunger; A salesman makes money because of a need or problem; A policeman makes money because of lawlessness; A doctor makes money because of ill health. Find a miserable situation and find a solution to make some money.

Signs of Workaholism

According to experts, long hours on the job don't necessarily mean you are a workaholic. Low self-esteem and the inability to relax trigger the addiction. The following are common characteristics of work addicts.

- Dependent on work for a feeling of importance.
- Loss of sleep due to thoughts about work.
- Fear of vacations, retirement or leisure.
- Ceaseless activity—working nights, weekends and holidays.
- Little contact with family or friends.
- Health jeopardized due to overwork.
- Depressed when idle.
- Failure to appreciate accomplishments.
- Inability to say no to working related requests.
- Parental history of work addiction. Legion 1983

Herbert P. Windschitl

You're Right

Yes, I'm tired. For a number of years I've been blaming it on old age, iron poor blood, lack of vitamins, air pollution, obesity, dieting, and a dozen other maladies that make you wonder if life is really worth living. Now I find out, tain't that. I'm tired because I'm overworked. The population of this country is some 200 million. Eighty-four million are retired. That leaves 116 million to do the work. There are 75 million in school which leaves 41 million to do the work. Of this total, there are 22 million employed by the government.

That leaves 19 million to do the work. Four million are in the Armed Forces, which leaves 15 million to do the work. Take from that total the 14,800,00 who work for State and City governments and that leaves 200,000 to do the work. There are 188,000 in hospitals, so that leaves 12,000 to do the work. Now there are 11,998 people in prison. That leaves just two people to do the work—**you and me.** And you're sitting there reading this. No wonder I'm tired. Anonymous

Anyway

People are unreasonable, illogical, and self centered—love them anyway! If you do good people will accuse you of selfish, interior motives—do good anyway! If you are successful you win false friends and true enemies—succeed anyway! The good you do today will be forgotten tomorrow—do good anyway! Honesty and frankness make you vulnerable—be honest and frank anyway! People favor underdogs, but follow only top dogs—fight for some underdogs anyway! What you spend years building may be destroyed overnight—build anyway! People really need help but may attack you if you help them—help them anyway! Give the world the best you have and you'll get kicked in the teeth—give the world the best you've got **<u>Anyway!</u>** Anonymous

Herbert P. Windschitl

Cardinal Cushing

Dear God; Help me to be a good sport in life. I don't ask for an easy place in the lineup. Put me anywhere you need me. I only ask that I can give you 100% of everything I have. If all the hard times seem to come my way, I thank you for the compliment. Help me remember that you never send a player more trouble than he can handle. And help me Lord to accept the bad breaks as part of the game. May I always play on the square, no matter what the others do. Help me study the Book so I'll know the rules. Finally God if the natural turn of events goes against me and I'm benched for sickness or old age, help me to accept that as part of the game too. Keep me from whimpering that I was framed or that I got a raw deal. And when I finish the final inning I ask for no laurels. All I want is to believe in my heart that I played as well as I could and that I didn't let you down.

Pax+Peace
Cross of Holy Father Benedict.
May the holy cross be my light.
Let the dragon not be my guide.
Begone Satan!
Never suggest evil things to me.
What you offer me is evil;
Drink the poison yourself!
Saint Benedict Medal words. Monte Cassino 1880.

I never met a student I didn't like. Sometimes it took awhile to find the best in them.

Be Honest under pressure.

Brevity is the soul of wit.

Try, try, try again.
Always come up trying or go down trying.

It is equally important to promote life after birth as it is to promote life after death.

Say what you mean and mean what you say.

For God's sake, give a little to help a lot. Dublin, Ireland

If Mary and Joseph were looking for a home for Jesus, would they choose your house and all it holds?

The spirit **wars** against the flesh.

Way Of The Flesh: Hurry up and get married so I can live in misery.

Way Of True Love: Develop a true wholesome relationship over a period of time so that you will live in harmony and happiness.

When you love someone you need to love him or her as they are.

We must live together as brothers or we will perish like fools.

What's the highest building in any city? Library—it has many stories.

We must decide between being a leader or being lead.

Show and tell is kindergarten mentality; Adult mentality is show and sell.

By man's creative work is his civilization measured. Ernest Leonard Painter

Don't do for others what they can do for themselves.

We either release the energies of the flesh or of the spirit.

1001 Affirmations

"The moving finger writes, and having writ moves on, and all your piety and all your wit cannot suffice to cancel out a line of it." Omar Khyam

What did you come up with? <u>That I'm more important than my problems.</u>

You first make your friends than your friends make you.

Abbey; You can't build happiness on the sorrow of others.

Hospice program—After death—don't feel guilty but ask yourself, What can I do now?

Avoid loud and aggressive persons. They are the vexations of the spirit.

Of all the things you wear, your expression is the most important. Janet Lane

Can you shift and move from one project or task to another as fast and smoothly as you like?

ON CONFLICTS; Let us sit down and take counsel together. Woodrow Wilson

Don't over react to problems or events or demands placed upon us.

What we are is God's gift to us; What we become is our gift to God.

Herbert P. Windschitl

Man is to live; Not prepare to live. Pasternak

Never Explain; Never complain. 3 decades in business. Henry Ford ll

In quietness and in trust shall be your strength.

If you do not understand my silence you will not understand my words.

Wisely and slowly they stumble that run fast.

Be a friend the rest will follow.

WCCO 1978 American Economic System. A right to succeed; A right to fail; A right to try; A right to start; A right to quite.

Don't criticize your wife's judgment—Look whom she married.

A child's mind does not keep library hours.

Parents do not plan for these children to fail—they simply fail to plan.

Children's minds are like grasshoppers—They hop from one subject to another.

Though we travel the world over to find the beautiful;
We must carry it with us or we will find it not.

Free knowledge M-F—Bring your own container.

Herbert P. Windschitl

Hurt must be examined. Poet Anne Sexton 1974

Home is not where you live, but where they understand you.

Walt Disney; You may not realize it when it happens, but a kick in the teeth may be the best thing in the world for you.

Don't ever do things just for money only. Be of service to other people and you will be of service to yourself.

Intelligent people talk about ideas; Average people talk about things; Small people talk about other people.

Smile—Even a grouch doesn't want to do business with a grouch.

"The tyranny of the should" holds us back from putting the most in our present time. Fr. Basset <u>Noonday Devil</u>

The Faith of God is always there.

The only thing that's important in life are your personal goals. Make these with thought and consideration. They will eventually make you or break you.

If you are too busy to pray; You are too busy. Remember that your God given soul is more important than anything else in life.

Herbert P. Windschitl

Those who have believed in the Lord at one time and who no longer believe are the deadest of the dead. Paul / Bible

Everyone at times has butterflies in his stomach. Make sure you use their full potential by flying them in formation.

When we get to the point of wanting a clean house more than wanting good books in the home; we are really going down hill.

Let us thank the Lord that he does not always give us what we want or deserve.

Control your life or <u>Life</u> will control you. Father to Loretta Lind.

Trickle down theory; Horse and sparrow theory. "If you feed a horse enough oats some will pass through to the sparrows on the road." Elections between Rich and the Poor.

No other business or organization in the world provides man with an eternal reward save that of the Church of Jesus Christ.

Spouses outlook; Catch someone doing some good today. Nastiness begets nastiness. Psychiatrist St. Paul paper. 1982

When another person throws a curve ball in the use of your language, how do you react? Positively or negatively.

The road to success is always under construction.

Sad indeed is the person who only uses money to judge success in life.

Six great ideas: Truth; Goodness; Beauty; Liberty; Justice; Equality.

Today is the tomorrow we worried about yesterday.

Let life happen.

Abbey in Texas; "Intimacy between man and woman is God's wedding gift to newly weds and his gift is not to be opened early."

Imitate greatness or we're doomed to create mediocrity.

Nothing is real until it comes locally. G. K. Chesterton

Everyone is a part of the whole picture. One family member—whole family; One worker—whole company; One member with belief in Christ—whole Church; One player on the team—becomes the whole team.

ASS U ME When you assume something you make an ass out of you and of me.

CHRISTOPHER'S: Better to light one candle than to curse the darkness.

Dig and be dug in return. Langston Hughes

Herbert P. Windschitl

Mother

The most important person on earth is a MOTHER. She has built something more magnificent than any cathedral—a dwelling for an immortal soul, the tiny perfection of her baby's body. The angels have not been blessed with such a grace. They cannot share God's creative miracle to bring new saints to heaven. Only a human mother can. Mothers are closer to God than any other creature; God joins forces with mothers in performing this act of creation. What on earth is more glorious than this; to be a mother?
Cardinal Mindszenty

Guide me on my way, Lord. I need not know the path. Just give me enough light to see the next step. Like a trusting child I will put my hand into your hand, my step into your step.

Challenges

Author Unknown
When things go wrong, as they sometimes will.
When the road you're trudging seems all uphill.
When the funds are low, and the debts are high.
And you want to smile, but can only sigh.
And your cares are pressing you down a bit.
It's when things seem worst that you mustn't quit.

Life is queer with its twists and turns.
As everyone of us sometimes learns.
And many a fellow turns about.
When he might have won, had he stuck it out.
So don't give up, though the pace seems slow.
You may succeed with the very next blow.

Often the goal is much nearer than
It would seem to a faint and faltering man.
Often the struggler has given up.
When he might have captured that victor's cup.
He learned too late, when night came down.
How close he was to that golden crown.

Success is failure turned inside out.
The silver tint of the clouds of doubt.
And you never can tell how close you are.
It may be near and yet seem so far.
So stick to the fight and when you're hardest hit.
Rest if you must, but don't you quit.

Herbert P. Windschitl

A Father's Prayer

Build me a son, O Lord, who will be strong enough to know when he is weak, and brave enough to face himself when he is afraid; one who will be proud and unbending in honest defeat, and humble and gentle in victory.

Build me a son who will know thee and that to know himself is the foundation stone of knowledge. Lead him, I pray, not in the path of ease and comfort, but under the stress and spur of difficulties and challenge. Here let him learn to stand up in the storm; here let him learn compassion for those who fail.

Build me a son whose heart will be clear, whose goal will be high; a son who will master himself before he seeks to lead others; one who will learn to laugh, yet never forget how to weep; one who will reach into the future, but never forget the past.

And after all these things are his, add I pray, enough of a sense of humor, so that he may always be serious, yet never take himself too seriously. Give him humility, so that he may always remember the simplicity of true greatness, the open mind of true wisdom and the meekness of true strength.

Then I, his father, will dare to whisper, "I have not lived in vain." General Douglas MacArthur

I do not desire riches for riches sake but only enough money to pay our bills and then some for family and favorite charities.

Birds of one feather flock together.

There can be no rainbow without a cloud and a storm.

Destiny is not a matter of chance, it is a matter of choice.

The greatest truths are the simplest.

They can because they think they can. A dreamer lives forever.

Speak kind words and you will hear kind echoes.

Happiness is like a butterfly—the more you chase it the more it eludes you.
But if you turn your attention to other things; It comes and softly sits on your shoulders.

Don't follow where the path leads, rather go where there is no path and leave a trail.

Colors speak all languages.

The deepest feelings show in silence.

You observe a lot by watching.

Herbert P. Windschitl

When the outlook is bad try looking up.

Serenity is not freedom from the storm, but peace amid the storm.

And it was good.

Happiness is found along the way, not at the end of the road.

If there were dreams to sell, what would you buy?

Happy are they who dream dreams and are ready to pay the price to make them come true.

Pope John II's Thoughts

Nowhere does Christ condemn the mere possession of earthly goods as such, "Instead, he pronounces very harsh words against those who use their possessions in a selfish way without paying attention to the needs of others." Lazarus of the 20th century stands at our doors. Riches and freedom create a special responsibility and special obligation.

"We must find a simple way of living—It is in the joyful simplicity of life inspired by the Gospel and the Gospels spirit of fraternal sharing that you will find the best remedy for sour criticism, paralyzing doubt and the temptation to make money the principal means and indeed the very measure of human advancement."

"Faced with problems and disappointments many people will try to escape from responsibility; escape in selfishness; escape in sexual pleasure; escape in drugs, escape in violence; escape in indifference and cynical attitudes. But today, I propose to you the option of love, which is the opposite of escape."

"Christ came to bring Joy," he said; "In a true sense, joy is the keynote of Christian message and recurring motif of the Gospels. But how many people have never known this joy?" The Pope asked, "They feed on emptiness and tread the paths of despair. They live in our neighborhoods, they walk down our streets, they may even be members of our families—They live without hope because families have never heard, really heard the good news of Jesus Christ, because they have never met a brother or sister who touched their lives with the love of Jesus and lifted them up from their misery."

Herbert P. Windschitl

"We must go to them therefore as messengers of hope. We must bring to them the witness of true joy. We must pledge to them our commitment to work for a just society where they feel respected and loved." *Wall Street Journal* 10/5/1979.

When you don't go to church, you court other god's of too much money, materialism, power and worldly concerns.

Home is where the heart is.

You cannot serve two masters.

When one door closes another opens; but we often look so long and so regretfully upon the closed door that we do not see the one which has been opened for us.
Alexander Graham Bell

Variety is the spice of life

Discretion is the better part of valor.

Herbert P. Windschitl

IT IS NEVER TOO SOON TO BE KIND, FOR WE NEVER KNOW HOW SOON IT WILL BE TOO LATE.

1001 Affirmations

CROSS A LINE ON THE OCEAN, YOU LOSE A DAY...

CROSS A LINE ON THE HIGHWAY, YOU CAN DO EVEN BETTER THAN THAT!

LIFE IS A RAT RACE.

THE REAL CHALLENGE IS IN LEARNING TO LIKE RAT RACING.

Herbert P. Windschitl

Seven Laws Of Success

Herb Armstrong 1986
1. Choosing the right vocational goal.
2. Acquiring the right knowledge.
3. Good health.
4. Drive.
5. Overcome obstacles by being resourceful.
6. Stick to it. Perseverance.
7. Personal contact with God's love. Find ways to Give not Get.

I've been beaten; kicked; lied to; cussed at; swindled; taken advantage of and laughed at so many times **but** The only reason I hang around this place is to see what happens next.

You lose sometimes and you win sometimes.

Committed & Involved: Ham and eggs breakfast. Chicken was involved but the pig was committed.

I'm at a point in life when someone calls me a loser; I look him in the eye and say "Look who's talking."

Computer age: Sad is the person who feels the computer replaces the human mind. Happy are others who find the computer removes the tedious tasks from the human mind and now finds more creative time to cultivate talents and abilities.

Religion wasn't necessarily a topic of conversation at our house—My Dad went to Mass often and when we had problems or troubles we went to confession. Perry Como

Education alone is useless unless it is applied to help man to improve himself and others.

There are only 3 kinds of people who don't own books: 1. The destitute; 2. The ones that don't like an educational advantage for their children; 3. The ones who haven't seen it. Which one are you?

At this point in time we cannot accept your view point because it does not meet our existing ideas about this subject.

Buying books
When your child is 2 months. Don't buy—Too young.
When your child is 3 years old. Don't buy—Too young.
When your child is 6 years old. Don't buy—Too young.
When your child is 10 years old. Don't buy—Too old.
When your child is 18 years old—Too late—Kiss your child goodbye.

The word discipline involves a bossy attitude in order to accomplish a set goal. Setting limits are words that essentially say the same but it involves freedom within a task or set goal.

Opportunity: Please knock more than once!!!—I may be out back taking the garbage out. Thank You. Ziggy

Man should learn from the chicken. See how she cares and gathers her young under her wing.

I like a finished speaker, not a polished speaker, but one who is thoroughly finished. The top speakers speak fast. WCCO

Learn to appreciate silence.

No man can survive unless he meets the demands of Love, Honor and Duty. Conrad "The Lagoon" English Literature.

A house divided against itself will not stand. Jesus

Lord forgive my enemies for they know not what they do.

God said it. I believe it. That settles it. Paul Harvey

Reach out and touch the reading life of a small child.

Sales Golden Rule: Treat people like you would like to be treated, with respect and dignity.

When opposites attract and they wed: Extrovert/introvert; Sensing/intuition; Thinking/feeling; Judging/perceiving. Carl Jung Psychiatrist

Three Challenges In Sales: Attitude, Enthusiasm and Service.

On Sales Excuses: Smile, Agree, Turn, Add more value and close.

The big ones are easier to sell.

Explain: Need, use and value; Create want.

Dig, Dig, Dig. Only through digging do we find gold and silver.

You influence people you get paid—You don't influence people you don't get paid.

Enthusiasm Is Developed: 1. Curiosity, 2. Interests, 3. Knowledge, 4. Belief.

Am I in a home where my presentation will sell the prospect, and if sold, can the prospect pay?

If children listened to everything parents told them they would turn into idiots or geniuses.

Overcoming objections in hiring
Feel—I know how you feel.
Felt—I also felt like that.
Found—But I found that experience showed me.

Herbert P. Windschitl

It's a strange challenging irony in our Democratic society that we must allow complete freedom of expression without censorship and at the same time we must challenge man's intellect to read and accept the best of man's thinking and avoid damaging ideas that deteriates society to a beastial level.

The Scoutmaster's Wife

Who answers the phone from dawn to dark
When the "little Scouts" go on a lark?
The Scoutmaster's wife!

Who usually sits and waits at home
While beside cool streams the Scouts all roam?
The Scoutmaster's wife!

Who helps him pack for a week at camp
And waves farewell from the highest ramp?
The Scoutmaster's wife!

But who else in the town has so many fine boys
And watches with interest their sorrows and joys?
The Scoutmaster's wife!

Some folks want great honors or riches from life,
I'd rather be just
The Scoutmaster's wife!
Mildred D. Goodwin

In Our Books
Herb Windschitl

In our books we seek the prayers of God and man.
In our books we seek our peace.
In our books we gain inspiration.
In our books we seek the words of God.
In our books we learn of lifes challenges.
In our books we move to change our ways.
In our books we keep our records.
In our books we see how husband and wife grow together.
In our books we see how to help our children grow.
In our books we seek ways to improve our health.
In our books we see man's destiny.
In our books we record our family as we grow.
Give me good books and a few old friends and family.
And I'll find my God to help steer my ship about.
Though the waters be rough or calm.
We'll match our wits with a repertorie of books.
For with a book's idea we can change the course of history.

Herbert P. Windschitl

Reaching out

Reach out to Him, the time for love is now. Nobody knows you better than He does. He always understands, no matter what. He's ready to forgive whatever it was. Reach out to Him, nor ever be afraid. Walk slowly 'lest you miss Him in your haste. Make Him a part of everything you do. For life was never given you to waste. Reach out to Him, and never be alone. Just as the sunlight filters through the trees, so shines His love throughout the darkest hours, sustaining us through moments such as these. It is in trusting Him above all else that we come to know what life is all about, and find a God who takes within His own…the hand we are forever reaching out.
—Grace E. Easley

Never too late to mend. Spanish

He was so broad minded his brains fell out or He was so narrow minded he became constipated.

Transcendental Meditation: Concentrate on one word. Put all else aside. Love; Family; Life; God; etc.

There is only one vocation in life, and that is being a good Christian.

What doth it profit a man if he gain the whole world and suffer the loss of his own soul.

St. Joseph: Little is said about him except that; "He was a just man."

God is faithful to his servants. They are rewarded; Not always in the light of man's thinking.

God grants intelligence but some never come to know the heart wherein all compassion grows.

Possible Sale. Give it all you got or if no possible sale, get out and save you mental attitude.

Either work to live or live to work.

"Knowledge is Power" Francis Bacon

JFK "I do not speak for my church on public matters and the church does not speak for me." He won nomination for the Presidency by separating powers. Minneapolis Tribune 1976.

Behold the Truth. He makes progress only when he sticks his neck out.

Man can make a set of books: but only God can make a child.

There's always one extra thing to do after you have done everything right.

The biggest oak was once a little nut that held its ground.

Be good to your children because some day they will be making decisions about you.

Nobody believes in you until you believe in yourself.

Life is full of surprises.

The art of a perfect life is the art of perfect giving.

You don't have to be crazy to work with us, but it helps.

I know you believe you understood what you think I said, but I am not sure you realize that what you heard is not what I meant.

Congratulations on your promotion; Nothing happens until someone sells something. With the demands placed upon us today to use our talents and abilities to the fullest— it's important that we do not let chance enter into the development of our talents.

Definition of salesmanship; If it's good for the person you can never be high pressure. If it's not good for you anything you do is high pressure.

They prayed together.

Be not ashamed to confess your sins. ECCL Bible

God and the penitent soul meet each other in a HOLY KISS. <u>Imitation of Christ</u>

Man does not live by bread alone, but by the word of God.

Jesus is the bridge over troubled water.

Listen to the teaching of the master and bend the ear of your heart. Rule of St. Benedict

What ever is important to you at this time becomes your God.

When you date someone you should keep in mind; "Would this person be a good mother or father some day for our children?"

Stop educational abuse. Buy the books kids can and will use.

Two shoe salesmen went to Africa to open up new territories. Three days after their arrival the first salesman sent a cable; "Returning on the next plane. Can't sell shoes here, everybody goes barefoot." Nothing was heard from the second salesman for about two weeks. Then came a fat airmail envelope with this message for the home office: "Fifty orders enclosed. Prospects unlimited. Nobody here has shoes." Robert Rich—

When I am right no one remembers. When I am wrong no one forgets.

The Almighty doesn't feed the birds. They have to go out and do their own scratching.

All the waters from the seven seas can't sink a ship unless it gets inside.

We can't live our lives entirely by the book. We must also live for and by the people we work with.

Jesus said: Success was not important but pleasing the Father was; LK 10 17,18-20 Obedience to the Father would merit them a reward; Mt. 12:47-50 His mother's glory was not in bearing and suckling Him but in her receiving and loving the word of God. LK 11:27,28

TAKE TIME

Take time to think;
    It is the source of power.
Take time to play;
It is the secret of perpetual youth.
Take time to read;
    It is the fountain of wisdom.
Take time to pray;
    It is the greatest power on earth
Take time to love and be loved;
    It is a God given privilege.
Take time to be friendly;
    It is the road to happiness.
Take time to laugh;
    It is the music of the soul.
Take time to give;
    It is too short a day to be selfish.
Take time to work;
    It is the price of success.
Take time to do charity;
    It is the key to heaven.

Herbert P. Windschitl

Prayer for Peace

Lead me from death to life.
From falsehood to truth.
Lead me from hate to love.

From war to peace.
Lead me from despair to hope.
From fear to trust.
Let peace fill our heart, our world.
OUR UNIVERSE.

Three types of friends; 1. "Hi friends" Everyone fits in this category. A God like image is in every man, woman and child. 2. "Business or working friends" Friendly because it means your bread and butter. You want good solid relationships here. 3. "Personal friends" You'd be willing to tell any personal feeling you have to this person. Our relationship to God would also fall into this category.

Time

Don't waste it. On this day mend a quarrel. Search out a forgotten friend. Dismiss a suspicion and replace it with trust. Encourage someone who has lost faith. Keep a promise. Forget an old grudge. Examine your demands on this and vow to reduce them. Fight for a principle. Express your gratitude. Overcome an old fear. Take two minutes to appreciate the beauty of nature. Tell someone you love him or her. Tell him again, and again and again. *Minneapolis Tribune 1983.*

Thanksgiving prayer: This Thanksgiving day let us thank God for our life, food, clothing and shelter and above all the friendships we share as a family. And Lord especially bless the people who have prepared this food.

Herbert P. Windschitl

Love

There is no difficulty that enough love will not conquer. No disease that enough love will not heal. No door that enough love will not open. No gulf that enough love will not bridge. No wall that enough love will not throw down. No sin that enough love will not redeem. It makes no difference how deeply seated may be the trouble; how hopeless the outlook; how muddled the tangle; how great the mistake. A sufficient realization of love will dissolve it all. If only you could have love enough you would be the happiest and most powerful being in the world.

The Bible is full of symbols; Sheep, lamb, dove, sword, money, whip, crowns, wells, wheat, trees, donkey, fields, seeds, pigs, blood, mustard seed, rocks, stones, ears, eye, cheek, grape, frogs, vine, locusts, weather, cross, treasurer, chrism, water, plants, flowers, garments, candles, chalice, cup, bread, lion, locusts, apple, snake, man.

We need one another. We love one another. We forgive one another. We work together. We play together. We worship together. Together we use God's word. Together we grow in Christ. Together we love all men. Together we serve our God. Together we hope for heaven. These are the hopes and ideals. Help us to attain them O God, through Christ our Lord.

1001 Affirmations

EVERYTHING HAS BEEN IMPROVED IN THIS YEAR'S MOTOR CARS...

...EXCEPT THE DRIVERS!

THERE ARE OLD DRIVERS AND BOLD DRIVERS, BUT THERE ARE VERY FEW OLD, BOLD DRIVERS.

Success

He has achieved success who has lived well, laughed often and loved much; who has enjoyed the truth of pure women, the respect of intelligent men and love of little children; who has filled his niche and accomplished his task; who has left the world a better place than he found it, whether by an improved poppy, a pretty poem or rescued soul; who has never lacked appreciation of earth's beauty or failed to express it; who has always looked for the best in others and given them the best he had; whose life was a inspiration; whose memory a benediction.
by Bessie Anderson Stanley 1905

The author's son, Arthur J. Stanley Jr., a senior judge of the U.S. district court in Leavenworth, Kansas has provided documentation from the Kansas State Historical Society that his mother is indeed the author.

Power corrupts and absolute power corrupts absolutely.
Lord Ackton

Herbert P. Windschitl

Alcohol Kills

A recent survey by the National Highway Traffic Safety Administration indicates that:

- 60% of dead drivers of cars, light trucks, vans or motorcyles had been drinking.
- 40% of dead pedestrians were intoxicated.
- 44% of dead pedestrians had some alcohol in their systems.

Alcohol's delusions
- We drank for joy and became miserable.
- We drank for sociability and became argumentative.
- We drank for sophistication and became obnoxious.
- We drank for friendship and made enemies.
- We drank for sleep and woke up exhausted.
- We drank for strength and felt weak.
- We drank to feel exhilaration and ended up depressed.
- We drank for "medicinal purposes" and acquired health problems.
- We drank to get calmed down and ended up with the shakes.
- We drank for confidence and became afraid.
- We drank to make conversation flow more easily and the words came out slurred and incoherent.
- We drank to diminish our problems and saw them multiply.
- We drank to cope with life and invited death.

Anonymous

Be Bold!!

I started out on a sales career when my well-meaning friends, with a good deal more doubt and cynicism than faith, were telling me to play it safe. I see them occasionally these days and they're still doing what they call "playing it safe"—they're still not sticking their necks out—their doubts have increased, but their achievements and well-being have not. Robert Dollar once made an unpopular but very perceptive statement. He said, "From above we can hear the crowd below growling and grumbling and taking it easy." Earl Night

Selling involves the attitude you have for your product: Fear, Shame, Guilt, Joy-pleasure, Sympathy, Competition, Desire, Success, Independence, Individuality, Comfort, Security, Popularity, Youth appeal, Convenience, Free time, Labor saving.

Consistent number of demonstrations plus a consistent mental attitude equals a consistent number of sales.

Important To A Salesperson: Rejection; What you say; How you sound; How many times do you say it; (Don't let the prospect wear you out; Be persistent) Who you call on (Look for ready buyers).

Herbert P. Windschitl

It is essential to be able to perceive where this crucial breakdown and break even point is so you know enough to quit and direct your energies in some other profitable direction. Don't over kill allowing other needed activities to remain undeveloped and unrealized.   Jim Thompson 1981

It's easier said than done.

When you get to the end of your rope tie a knot and hang on.

Jealousy creeps in when there is no understanding of the situation.

Be An Angel

Reach for the stars.
Share you favorite things with others.
Keep your halo polished.
Show respect for older people.
Always mind your manners.
Make friends with someone who is shy.
Plant a garden for butterflies.
Say a nice thing to someone every day.
Never make fun of anyone.
Make your bed every morning.
Talk to plants to help them grow.
Think happy thoughts.
Don't make too much noise when flapping your wings.
Clean up after yourself.
Clean up after others.
Donate a part of your allowance to a worthy cause.
Always tell the truth.
Be patient with those who don't fly as fast as you do.
Sprinkle a little stardust wherever you go.
Unknown author

A strong self image is the best preparation for success in life. Dr. Joyce Brothers

P. E. Department On Stress Control: 1. Get more sleep, 2. Eat healthier, 3. Exercise 10-15 minutes a day, 4. Breathe deeply, 5. Pray more fervently.

Herbert P. Windschitl

Ten secrets to success and inner peace

Dr. Wayne Dyer MPR 2002. 1. They have an open mind to everything and attached to nothing; 2. You can't give away what you don't have; 3. There are no justified resentments; 4. Don't die with your music still in you; 5. Embrace silence; 6. Give up personal history; 7. You can't solve the problem with the same mind that created it; 8. Treat yourself like you already have it; 9. Treasure your divinity; 10. Wisdom is avoiding all thoughts that weaken.

If you think a cluttered desk is indicative of a cluttered mind, what are you to think when you have an empty desk?

Did he know Christ so that a church could claim him for a christian burial.

Family Affirmations

I'm in heaven with a boat and fishing pole. Albert Meidl

Knitting Afghans keeps me busy and helps each one in the family to keep warm and comfortable. Leona Meidl

The family that prays together stays together. Fr. Peyton

Just what part of no don't you understand the "N" or "O" Mike

When the going gets rough and dangerous I can climb a pole faster then you can. Pat

Climbing mountains and camping with the family are exhilarating activities. Pat

The joy of cooking is a motherly activity that gets to the stomach of kids and adults. Bernie

Two wrongs don't make a right. Bernie

Quilting activities creates a strong imagination and bonding relationship. Julie and Rose

The home schooling spirit has given us many great men and women. Candy

Family camping is a great family activity. Herb and Bernie Windschitl

Herbert P. Windschitl

If you love something, set it free. If it comes back, it's yours. If it doesn't, it never was. Jane

Cross country skiing and Tour'd Saints with a 50 mile bike ride challenges the best of us. Mike & Rose

A piece of land with peace and quiet is my terra firma. Julie Ann

Some basket ball skills help to keep a restaurant manager on his toes. Gary

A catered to relative is a friend indeed and worth a pound of gold. Kim

The world runs with numbers. Fran

I'll give you 10 minutes of my time and then I need to make a living. Brian

You can tell we love running. The many 26 mile marathons keep Jane and Jon on the go.

The first step in being able to do anything is to believe you can. Jon

The iron man triathlon challenges the best of us. Jon

Be a strong person; a child of God; and a loving person. Florian and Anna Windschitl

Love your work and keep moving on. Florian and Anna Windschitl & John and Gertrude Windschitl

In manus tuas Domine, Comendo spiritum meum.
BIBLE.

Dearest Lord, teach me to be generous;
teach me to serve You as You deserve: to give
and not to count the cost, to fight and not to
heed the wounds, to toil and not to seek for
rest, to labor and not to ask for reward save
that of knowing I am doing Your will.
St. Ignatius Loyola

Lord, make me an instrument of Your Peace:
Where there is hatred, let me sow love;
Where there is injury, pardon;
Where there is doubt, faith;
Where there is despair, hope;
Where there is darkness, light;
Where there is sadness, joy.
O Divine Master, grant that I may seek not so
much to be consoled as to console; to be understood as to understand; to be loved as to love;
for it is in giving that we receive; it is in pardoning that we are pardoned, and it is in dying that
we are born to Eternal Life. Amen. **St. Francis**

Herbert P. Windschitl

Goal Setting

Set goals in the six areas of your life. Spiritual; Mental; Physical; Social; Financial; Family and if in business Organizational goals.

Use 3x5 cards to make it CONVENIENT to read and reread your goals.

Set goals or a purpose in life with short range (Now) and long range goals (5-10 years or lifetime.)

Attitude is a little thing that makes a big difference. You can change the world.

"Whatever you vividly imagine, ardently desire, sincerely believe, and enthusiastically act upon—must inevitably come to pass!" Paul J. Meyer

State your general goals & purpose of **What do I want out of life?** in 100 words or less.

Make a master dream list.

Make a visualization chart of your goals.

Make an affirmation list to keep you on track to achieve your goals.

Have a list of **Goals Achieved** to help you see what you said you're going to do. Set some tangible goals that you can see.

Remember any goal set always has some **obstacles & roadblocks**. With these have your **solutions** listed.

Have a specific target date to complete this goal.

List your rewards personally and for those people around you.

Keep a progress chart as to how you're doing to achieve your goal or purpose.

Herbert P. Windschitl

Authors motto and leaders prayer

MY MOTTO: FOREVER DISSATISFIED WITH THE STATUS QUO. ALWAYS IMPROVING AND BEING A BETTER PERSON. ALWAYS DO SOMETHING TO ACHIEVE YOUR PURPOSE OR GOAL. GOD WILL PROVIDE.

FORWARD: THE CLIMB TO THE TOP OF THE MOUNTAIN IS A HARD AND ARDUOUS TASK. WHEN WE'RE THERE, THE LONELINESS CROWDS IN AROUND US, AND THE WINDS OF CONFUSION BLOW FROM ALL DIRECTIONS.

LEADERS PRAYER

GOD THE FATHER, GRANT US THE POWER AND INSIGHT TO DEVELOP OURSELVES WITH STRONG CHARACTER TRAITS, AND THAT, THAT STRENGTH MIGHT RADIATE TO OTHERS, MAKING A BETTER WORLD IN WHICH TO LIVE UNDER CHRIST'S HUMAN AND DIVINE LEADERSHIP. GUIDE US, HOLY SPIRIT, TO DEVELOP OURSELVES SPIRITUALLY, MENTALLY, PHYSICALLY, SOCIALLY, FINANCIALLY AND FAMILY FOR THE HONOR AND GLORY OF GOD REALIZING THAT BY SERVING MAN WE ARE ALSO SERVING GOD. SHARING THE RIGHT ANSWERS, QUESTIONS AND EXPERIENCES HELPS MAN TO ACHIEVE THE HIGHEST GOAL OF ETERNITY AND EVERLASTING LIFE WITH GOD.
IN THE NAME OF JESUS WE PRAY. AMEN.

This prayer was ten years in the making (1972-1982). Only through the guidance of the Holy Spirit in the Holy Roman Catholic Church could I share this prayer with you.
Herbert P. Windschitl, Cold Spring, Minnesota

WHAT DO I WANT OUT OF LIFE? (100 WORDS OR LESS)

Herbert P. Windschitl

My Personal Goals

NAME_____ DATE_____

SUCCESS IS THE PROGRESSIVE REALIZATION OF WORTHWHILE PREDETERMINED PERSONAL GOALS.

Record your short and long range goals on 3x5 cards for easy access to read & reread your personal goals. Change them only under serious consideration.

GOALS OR PURPOSE

RANGE	SHORT	LONG
1. SPIRITUAL	X	XX
2. MENTAL	X	XX
3. PHYSICAL	X	XX
4. SOCIAL	X	XX
5. FINANCIAL	X	XX
6. FAMILY	X	XX
7. ORGANIZATION	X	XX

Celebrity And Author Affirmations

I take a simple view of life: keep your eyes open and get on with it. Lawrence Olivier

Democracy is the recurrent suspicion that more than half of the people are right more than half the time. E. B. White

At the touch of love, everyone becomes a poet. Plato

Change comes when someone sees the next step. William Drayton

Mondays are the potholes of life. Tom Wilson

Keep trying. It's only from the valley that the mountains seems high.

If your ship doesn't come in swim out to it. Jonathon Winters

Experience is what you get when you don't get what you want. Dan Stanford

Once you get people laughing they're listening and you can tell them almost anything. Herb Gardner

Any fool can criticize, condemn and complain—and most do. Dale Carnegie

It takes a long time to grow an old friend. John Leonard

Herbert P. Windschitl

Trust in God—but tie your camel tight. Persian Proverb.

There ain't no surer way to find out whether you like people or hate them than to travel with them. Mark Twain

A people that values its privileges above its principles soon loses both. Dwight D. Eisenhower

A warm smile is the universal languge of kindness. William A. Ward.

Everywhere is walking distance if you have the time. Steven Wright

The most important thing in communication is to hear what isn't being said. Peter F. Drucker

Happiness is conscious choice not an automatic response. Mildred Barthel

Time has a wonderful way of weeding out the trivial. Richard Ben Sapir

You don't have to suffer to be a poet. Adolescence is enough suffering for anyone. John Ciardi

Until you make peace with who you are, you'll never be content with what you have. Doris Mortman

You can't act like a skunk without someone getting wind of it. Lorene Workman

The arm of the moral universe is long, but it bends toward justice. Martin Luther King, Jr.

Discoveries are often made by not following instructions by going off the main road, by trying the untried. Frank Tyger

One famous musician reflected that if he misssed one day of practice he noticed it; if he missed two days his wife noticed it; if he missed three days his audience noticed it.

The hours that make us happy make us wise. John Masefield

Money is a good servant but a bad master. French Proverb

Christmas is the day that holds time together. Alexander Smith

This summer one third of the nation will be ill-housed and ill-nourished and ill-clad. Only they call it a vacation. Joseph Salak

A successful marriage requires falling in love many times, always with the same person. Mignon McLaughlin

The impersonal hand of government can never replace the helping hand of a neighbor. Hubert Humphrey

Fatherhood is pretending the present you love most is soap on a rope. Bill Crosby

A house without books is like a room without windows. Hoarce Mann

A leading authority is anyone who has guessed right more than once. Frank Clark

For the resolute and determined there is time and opportunity. Emerson

Make no judgments where you have no compassion. Anne McCaffrey

All serious daring starts from within. Eudora Welty

Education's purpose is to replace an empty mind with an open one. Malcolm Forbes

If you can spend a perfectly useless afternoon in a perfectly useless manner, you have learned how to live. Lin Yutang

Tact is rubbing out another's mistake instead of rubbing it in. Unknown

Those who flee temptation generally leave a forwarding address. Lane Olinghouse

One man practicing sportsmanship is far better than 50 preaching it. Knute K. Rockne

We find comfort among those who agree with us—growth among those who don't. Frank Clark

You never know when you're making a memory. Rickie Lee Jones

A ship in harbor is safe—but that is not what ships are for. John A. Shedd

To think too long about doing a thing often becomes its undoing. Eva Young

I like the word indolence. It makes my laziness seem classy. Bern Williams

A signature always reveals a man's character—and sometimes even his name. Evan Esar

The more you pass on to others, the more you keep for yourself.

The right thing to do something does not mean that doing it is right. William Safire

Expect the best. Prepare for the worst. Capitalize on what comes.

To err is human—and to blame it on a computer is even more so. Orben's current comedy

If things go wrong, don't go with them. Roger Babson

Marriage is like an army. Everybody complains, but you'd be surprised at how many re-enlist. The fortune cookie

By the time a man realizes that maybe his father was right he usually has a son who thinks he's wrong. Charles Wadsworth

The nice thing about teamwork is that you always have others on your side. Margaret Carty

People don't plan to fail, they just fail to plan.

English law probihits a man from marrying his mother-in-law. This is our idea of a useless legislation. Unknown

Whether you think you can or think you can't—you are right.

Treat a child as though he already is the person he's capable of becoming. Haim Ginott

Learning isn't a means to an end; it is an end in itself. Robert A Heinlein

Just remember, that when you're over the hill, you begin to pick up speed. Charles Schulz

Statistics are no substitute for judgment. Henry Clay

Other things may change us, but we start and end with family. Anthony Brandt

Standing in the middle of the road is very dangerous; you get knocked down by the traffic from both sides. Margaret Thatcher

Age does not diminish the extreme disappointment of having a scoop of ice cream fall from the cone. Jin Fiebig

A politician is a person who can make waves and then make you think he's the only one who can save the ship. Ivern Ball

What some people mistake for the high cost of living is really the cost of living high. Doug Larson

The cat could very well be man's best friend but would never stoop to admitting it. Doug Larson

Sometimes the fool who rushes in gets the job done. Al Bernstein

Luck is a matter of preparation meeting opportunity. Opray Winfrey

The best way to pay for a lovely moment is to enjoy it. Richard Bach

Cherishing children is the mark of a civilized society. Joan Ganz Cooney

Herbert P. Windschitl

Ideas are like rabbits. You get a couple and learn how to handle them and pretty soon you have a dozen. John Steinbeck

A true friend is someone who is there for you when he'd rather be anywhere else. Len Wein

I'm opposed to millionaires, but it would be dangerous to offer me the position. Mark Twain

In times like these, it helps to recall that there have always been times like these. Paul Harvey

Two important things are to have a genuine interest in people and to be kind to them. Kindness, I've discovered is everything in life. Issac Bashevis Singer

April hath put a spirit of youth in everything. William Shakepeare

An egotist is a person of low taste, more interested in himself than in me. Ambrose Bierce

If you had your life to live over again—you'd need more money.

If people concentrated on the really important things in life, there'd be a shortage of fishing poles. Doug Larson

The principal mark of genius is not perfection, but originality, the opening of new frontiers. Arthur Koestler

We may not imagine how our lives could be more frustrating and complex—but Congress can. Cullen Hightower

Show me a man who is a good loser and I'll show you a man who is playing golf with his boss. Nebraska Smoke Eater.

Spring is God's way of saying one more time. Robert Orben

Life is a great big canvas, and you should throw all the paint on it you can. Danny Kaye

He that can have patience can have what he will. Ben Franklin

Trying to squash a rumor is like trying to unring a bell. Shana Alexander

The entire sum of existence is the magic of being needed by just one person. Vil Putnam

I will say this about being an optimist—even when things don't turn out you are certain they will get better.

Love cures people—both the ones who give and the ones who receive it. Dr. Karl Menninger

I think of life as a good book. The further you get into it, the more it begins to make sense. Harold S. Kusher

There is no such thing as a nonworking mother. Hester Mundis

Few people are successful unless a lot of other people want them to be. Charles Brower

Some people march to a different drummer—and some PEOPLE polka. Unknown

We must accept finite disappointment, but we must never lose infinite hope. Martin Luther King Jr

Children are likely to live up to what you believe of them. Lady Bird Johnson

Be like a postage stamp—stick to one thing until you get there. Josh Billings.

In the race for quality, there is no finish line. David T. Kearns

No one has listened himself out of a job. Calvin Coolidge

Spring appears and we are once more children.

It is a funny thing about life; if you refuse to accept anything but the best, you very often get it. W. Somerset Maugham

To live only for some future goal is shallow. It's the sides of the mountain that sustain life, not the top. Robert M. Pirsig

Ignorance doesn't kill you, but it makes you sweat a lot. Haitian Proverb

In the matters of conscience, the law of majority has no place. Mohandas K. Gandhi

The best cure for insomnia is a Monday morning. Sandy Cooley

Hospitality is making your guests feel at home, even though you wish they were.

When a man's willing and eager, the gods join in. Aeschylus

There is no greater loan than a sympathetic ear. Frank Tyger

The greatest natural resource that any country can have is its children. Danny Kaye

You are better off not knowing how sausages and laws are made. Unknown

The explanation of triumph is all in the first syllable.

A goal properly set is half way reached.

Herbert P. Windschitl

You can finish school; you can even make it easy. That's not true education. You never finish it and it is seldom easy.

Winners evaluate themselves in a positive manner and look for their strengths as they work to overcome weaknesses. Zig Ziglar

One of the rarest things a man ever does is to do the best he can. Henry Wheeler Shaw

The Preamble To The Constitution

We the people of the United States, in order to form a more perfect union, establish justice, insure domestic tranquility, provide for the common defense, promote the general welfare, and secure the blessings of liberty to ourselves and our posterity, do ordain and establish this constitution for the United States of America.

My Dream List

1001 Affirmations

MOTTO

Forever dissatisfied with the status quo. Always improving and being a better person. Always do something to achieve your purpose or goal.

GOD WILL PROVIDE.

Herbert P. Windschitl

Your Directions

Your Personal Goals

Write on the kind of person you would like to be. What do you want out of life? (In 100 words or less.)

Herbert P. Windschitl

List Your Personal Affirmations And Goals

Or Goals Accomplished

#1   My Personal Affirmations And Goals.

#2 My Personal Affirmations And Goals.

Herbert P. Windschitl

#3 My Personal Affirmations And Goals.

… #4 My Personal Affirmations And Goals.

Herbert P. Windschitl

#5 My Personal Affirmations And Goals.

#6 My Personal Affirmations And Goals.

Herbert P. Windschitl

#7 My Personal Affirmations And Goals.

1001 Affirmations

J. Weston Walch

If you don't have time to do it right the first time, when do you expect to have time to do it over.

Caution: Plug in brain before starting mouth.

I'm a great believer in luck-but the harder I work, the more luck I seem to have.

The man who wakes up and finds himself famous hasn't been asleep.

Your opportunity is now—not tomorrow.

When all else fails read the instructions.

Be alert—Be on guard.

The problem is, I don't know what the problem is.

Buddha means enlightened one. He had four visions. Aging, Sickness, Death, and a holy man with religious enlightenment.

Buddhist wheel of life has 8 spokes. DHARMA Teaching. Frank Reynolds

1. Knowledge of truth.
2. The intentions to resist evil.
3. Saying nothing to hurt others.
4. Respecting life, morality and property.
5. Holding a job that does not injure others.
6. Striving to free one's mind of evil.
7. Controlling ones feelings and thoughts.
8. Practicing proper forms of concentration.

The quest for excellence is a life long process.

Have you used your brain today?

Learn from the past; Live in the present; Plan for the future.

The trick about life is to make it look easy.

Our nation runs and survives with the use of the wheel and axle.

Helen Keller was asked, "Is their anything worse than losing your sight?" Helen replied. "Yes there is, losing your vision is worse."

When the children are gone from the nest it's hard to relinquish your time in the sun as parents and to allow others to become the king of the hill.

There are no secrets to success. It is the result of preparation, hard work, and learning from failure. General Colin Powell

We all live under the same sky, but we don't reach for the same stars.

Work is a slice of your life. It's not the entire pizza.

When there is a hill to climb, don't think waiting will make it smaller.

Winning isn't always finishing first. Sometimes winning is just finishing.

Champions aren't born. They are made.

No kindness, no matter how small is ever wasted. Aesop

Let the choices you make today be choices you can live with tomorrow.

I believe in a division of labor even in the home.

Sometimes a spouse is someone you can't get along with, and someone you can't get along without.

There are times when too much togetherness doesn't help our situation.

Herbert P. Windschitl

The Best Gifts To Give

To your friend- loyalty.
To your enemy- forgiveness.
To your boss- service.
To a child- a good example.
To your parent- gratitude and devotion.
To your mate- love and faithfulness.
To all men and women- charity.
And to God- your life.
Kris Nelson 2002.

Religious Way Of Life: Poverty, Chastity and Obedience.

Citadel Military Academy's code just nine words.
"A cadet does not lie, or cheat nor steal."

In Physics: For every action there is an equal amount of reaction.

Take the bull by the horns.

Time will tell all.

Recognition is a cure for many ills.

Sometimes too much knowledge prevents new discoveries.

There is no such thing as a 50-50% marriage: It's all 100-00%; 00-100%.

<u>The Spiritual Craft</u>. The Bible; The Divine Office; The Holy Rosary; The Catechism; The Lives Of the Saints; Personal Prayers; Love God And Love Neighbor.

Celibacy is a fact of life in a religious setting. When stretching its definition, married couples are celibate at times and they are always celibate with men and women they work with on a daily basis.

No matter how much a man wishes to participate in the birth of a child, he can't. The birth is only between the mother and her view of God. If the mother has a poorly formed view of God she aborts. If she truly loves God a child is born.

PARENTS RULES

1. If you open it, **close it.**
2. If you turn it on, **turn it off.**
3. If you unlock it, **lock it again.**
4. If you break it, **repair it.**
5. If you can't fix it, **call in someone who can.**
6. If you borrow it, **return it.**
7. If you use it, **take care of it.**
8. If you make a mess, **clean it up.**
9. If you move it, **put it back.**
10. If it belongs to someone else, **get permission to use it.**
11. If you don't know how to operate it, **leave it alone.**
12. If it doesn't concern you, **leave it alone.**

Do what you think is best.

Herbert P. Windschitl

If you expect respect be the first to show it.

If you think no one cares think again.

When going through hell, just keep on going.
Winston Churchill.

Make every choice count, you don't always have a second chance.

There is no victory without honor.
Michael Josephson

Damned if you do; Damned if you don't.

It isn't fair but who said it's suppose to be fair.

Time can serve us well. We either live in the past, present of future. We need them all to fully enjoy life. Jesus is the same yesterday, now and coming days.

I may be over the hill, but I'm not under the hill yet.

I'd like to be buried in the forest where
my husband can hunt for me.

Keep your focus when living out your goals.

I believe in the death penalty because no one gets
out of life alive.

He wants to die with his boots on.

We have to take it with a grain of salt.

Don't throw the baby out with the wash water.

If you want it done right, do it yourself.

When it's built they'll come.

Not too bad.

Some people know the price of everything,
but little of its value. Bishop Sheen

Reading makes a full person; Conference a ready person;
Writing an accurate person; Listening a human person.
Crafty persons hold studies in contempt; Simple persons
admire them; Wise persons use them.

Herbert P. Windschitl

Politics is the art of pleasing 51% of the people
while ticking off 49% of the people to get
some appreciable good done for society.
The art of politics is for the necessary
good of society and not a necessary
evil. Good politicians help our society to grow for the
betterment of mankind as a whole.

I saw a crowd go down the street, and I need
to get in front of them, so I can lead.

No news generally means good news.

You said a mouth full.

Tense Conversation: Listen, acknowledge,
nod and ignore.

One drink is too much and 100 drinks are
not enough.

Is this the best use of my time now.

Money is a form of communication.

Better late than never roads.

Notice
This department requires no physical fitness program.
Everyone gets enough exercise by jumping to
conclusions; Flying off the handle; Running down
the boss; Knifing friends in the back;
Dodging responsibilities
by passing the buck.

On the flip side of this issue we see another view.

Do the known before you do the unknown.

Money has no power. You have power over
your money. Orman

The devil is in the details.

Writing is just printed talk.

Herbert P. Windschitl

Kids soon learn how to get your goat.

Do not get mad, get organized.

Open a life and come alive to smell the roses.

"I pledge allegiance to the Flag of the United States of America, and to the Republic for which it stands, one Nation under God, indivisible, with liberty and justice for all."

Snafu; Situation normal all fouled up.

At times we need to think outside the box of ordinary thinking.

Groucho Marx once said, "Politics is the art of looking for trouble, finding it, misdiagnosing it and then misapplying the wrong remedies."

Once kids get wheels under them they seem to be gone like a bird from a nest.

Sometimes we develop a love-hate relationship with those around us.

Why did God make me? God made me to know Him, to love Him, to serve Him in this world and to be happy with Him forever in the next.

We are all strangers at one time.

Success and failure are two imposters we need to treat them just the same.

We'll draw a line in the sand.

There are two kinds of workers in our society, the white collar worker and the blue collar worker. We need to respect them both in order to help us survive.

A salesman was asked why he always answered a question with a question. He replied, "Why shouldn't I?"
Fred Herman

If you had a good meal today thank a farmer.

He dug himself into a hole so deep he could no longer get out.

This is top of the line.

We need to draw a line.

Bottom Line.

Herbert P. Windschitl

Appendix

1001 Affirmations

Children Learn What They Live With

If a child lives with CRITICISM,
  he learns to CONDEMN.

If a child lives with HOSTILITY,
  he learns to FIGHT.

If a child lives with FEAR,
  he learns to be APPREHENSIVE.

If a child lives with PITY,
  he learns to feel SORRY FOR HIMSELF.

If a child lives with RIDICULE,
  he learns to be SHY.

If a child lives with JEALOUSY,
  he learns to feel GUILTY.

If a child lives with TOLERANCE,
  he learns to be PATIENT.

If a child lives with ENCOURAGEMENT,
  he learns to be CONFIDENT.

If a child lives with PRAISE,
  he learns to be APPRECIATIVE.

If a child lives with ACCEPTANCE,
  he learns to LOVE.

If a child lives with APPROVAL,
  he learns to LIKE HIMSELF.

If a child lives with RECOGNITION,
  he learns it is good to HAVE A GOAL.

If a child lives with HONESTY,
  he learns what TRUTH is.

If a child lives with FAIRNESS,
  he learns JUSTICE.

If a child lives with SECURITY,
  he learns to have FAITH IN HIMSELF
  and THOSE ABOUT HIM.

If a child lives with FRIENDLINESS,
  he learns that the
  WORLD IS A NICE PLACE IN WHICH TO LIVE.

With what is your child living?

Dorothy Low Nolte

Herbert P. Windschitl

All I really need to know
I learned in Kindergarten   Robert Fulghum

All I really need to know about how to live and what to do and how to be I learned in Kindergarten. Wisdom was not at the top of the graduate-school mountain, but there is a sandpile at Sunday School. These are the things I learned. Share everything. Play fair. Don't hit people. Put things back where you found them. Clean up your own mess. Don't take things that aren't yours. Say you're sorry when you hurt somebody. Wash your hands before you eat. Flush. Warm cookies and cold milk are good for you. Live a balanced life. Learn some and think some and draw and paint and sing and dance and play and work everyday some. Take a nap every afternoon. When you go out into the world, watch out for traffic, hold hands and stick toegether. Be aware of wonder. Remember the little seed in the styrofoam cup. The root goes down and the plant goes up and nobody really knows how or why, but we all like that. Goldfish and hamsters and white mice and even the little seed in the styrofoam cup -- they all die. So do we. And then remember the Dick and Jane books and the first word you learned. The biggest word of all <u>LOOK.</u> Everything you need to know is there somewhere. The GOLDEN RULE AND LOVE and basic sanitation. Ecology and politics and equality and some living. Take any of these items and extropolate it into sophisticated adult terms and apply it to your family life or your work, or your government or your world and it holds true and clear and firm. Think what a better world it would be if all -the whole world- had cookies and milk about three o clock every afternoon and then lay down with our blankets for a nap. Or if all governments had as a basic policy to always put things back where they found them and to clean up their own mess. And it is still true, no matter how old you are -when you go out into the world, it is best to hold hands and stick together.

DESIDERATA

GO PLACIDLY AMID THE NOISE & HASTE, & REMEMBER WHAT PEACE THERE MAY BE IN SILENCE. AS FAR AS POSSIBLE WITHOUT surrender be on good terms with all persons. Speak your truth quietly & clearly; and listen to others, even the dull & ignorant; they too have their story. ❧ Avoid loud & aggressive persons, they are vexations to the spirit. If you compare yourself with others, you may become vain & bitter; for always there will be greater & lesser persons than yourself. Enjoy your achievements as well as your plans. ❧ Keep interested in your own career, however humble; it is a real possession in the changing fortunes of time. Exercise caution in your business affairs; for the world is full of trickery. But let this not blind you to what virtue there is; many persons strive for high ideals; and everywhere life is full of heroism. ❧ Be yourself. Especially, do not feign affection. Neither be cynical about love; for in the face of all aridity & disenchantment it is perennial as the grass. ❧ Take kindly the counsel of the years, gracefully surrendering the things of youth. Nurture strength of spirit to shield you in sudden misfortune. But do not distress yourself with imaginings. Many fears are born of fatigue & loneliness. Beyond a wholesome discipline, be gentle with yourself. ❧ You are a child of the universe, no less than the trees & the stars; you have a right to be here. And whether or not it is clear to you, no doubt the universe is unfolding as it should. ❧ Therefore be at peace with God, whatever you conceive Him to be, and whatever your labors & aspirations, in the noisy confusion of life keep peace with your soul. ❧ With all its sham, drudgery & broken dreams, it is still a beautiful world. Be careful. Strive to be happy. ❧ ❧

FOUND IN OLD SAINT PAUL'S CHURCH, BALTIMORE; DATED 1692

About the Author

The author was born and raised along with five siblings on the prairie lands of Leavenworth, Minnesota, the home of the Church of the Japanese Martyrs, in the Springfield and Sleepy Eye area. After serving in the U.S. Army Engineers in Pusan, Korea, he graduated from St. John's University and did some graduate work at Mankato State University. He was a teacher for 14 years, directed 15 class plays and substituted for 26 years in Minnesota schools. He has worked with over 250,000 students. He and his wife Bernetta, presently live in Cold Spring, Minnesota where they raised a family of five boys and a girl. As a sales manager he sold 2000 sets of World Book Encyclopedias and related products and hired 200 sales people.

CPSIA information can be obtained
at www.ICGtesting.com
Printed in the USA
LVHW091424020820
662186LV00003B/6/J